Masked by Trust

Masked by Trust

Bias in Library Discovery

Matthew Reidsma

Published in 2019 by Litwin Books.

Litwin Books
PO Box 188784
Sacramento, CA 95818

http://litwinbooks.com/

This book is printed on acid-free paper.

Library of Congress Cataloging-in-Publication Data

Names: Reidsma, Matthew, author.
Title: Masked by trust : bias in library discovery / Matthew Reidsma.
Description: Sacramento, CA : Library Juice Press, 2019. | Includes
   bibliographical references and index.
Identifiers: LCCN 2019010995 | ISBN 9781634000833 (acid-free paper)
Subjects: LCSH: Information retrieval--Social aspects. | Search
   engines--Programming. | Online library catalogs. | Information storage and
   retrieval systems. | Filter bubbles (Information filtering) | Electronic
   information resource searching.
Classification: LCC ZA3075 .R445 2019 | DDC 025.5/24--dc23
LC record available at https://lccn.loc.gov/2019010995

Table of Contents

Acknowledgments

This book wouldn't have been possible without the support of countless others. First and foremost, I want to thank my colleagues at Grand Valley State University (GVSU) Libraries, who enthusiastically supported my research and the sabbatical that made this book possible. I am indebted to Patrick Roth, Mary Morgan, Matt Schultz, and Kyle Felker for early conversations on the research; Matt Ruen for his careful eye on author contracts, and his support for negotiating the 2-year open access embargo; Debbie Morrow and Kim Ranger for sending me a steady stream of news clippings on higher education and algorithms; Anna White for helping me wrangle my citations; and Hazel McClure for helping me refine the title of this project, for help shaping my sabbatical proposal, and for coffee and friendship throughout the years.

This project was inspired by the work of a number of librarians and other scholars, including Safiya Umoja Noble, Sara Wachter-Boettcher, Andromeda Yelton, Virginia Eubanks, Sara T. Roberts, and many of the discussions on Twitter under the #critlib hashtag. I also had important conversations with many colleagues outside of GVSU as I began the research. Without Annette Bailey of Virginia Tech's thoughtful advice and thorough knowledge of the technical infrastructure of Summon, this project would never have gotten off the ground. I also owe Cody Hanson, Pete Coco, Anglea Galvan, Matt Borg, Jason Clark, Carrie Moran, and Andreas Orphanides for their time and feedback.

I want to thank the members of the Summon Clients listserv, especially Ruth Kitchin Tillman of Penn State University Libraries, for sharing problematic examples and user and librarian experiences around incorrect and biased results. These library technologists could just submit tickets to Ex Libris in private, but the community works together to share issues and successes, and I am grateful to have been a member for the past eight years.

I also owe a debt to Brent Cook, the Summon Project Manager at Ex Libris, for patiently answering my many questions about the algorithms behind their discovery system, and for working to improve the system. I may not always agree with the way Ex Libris approaches improving their systems, but I have deep respect for Brent and his team. I also want to thank Deirdre Costello and Andrew Nagy for agitating within EBSCO for my research. I am eternally grateful to Eric Frierson for patiently answering my questions and walking me through EDS's interface and API, and for granting me access to their system when they knew I was looking for problems and issues.

The library community has also been extremely supportive of my work. I want to thank Andy Priestner of the UX Libs Conference, for inviting me to speak in Glasgow about the ethics of our technological processes in libraries. Brian Zelip, Sara Stephenson, and Nini Beegan invited me to speak at MD Tech Connect about user experience and how ethics plays a role in our work. Philip Dudas of the Minnesota Library Association also gave me a venue for sharing my work on ethics. And the attendees of the 2018 Code4Lib Annual Conference in Washington D.C. graciously accepted my proposal to speak about the technical side of researching algorithmic systems in libraries.

In all of this, my family supported me when I needed quiet space to write or read. But the most important thing they did was give me perspective and pull me away from both the negative and positive aspects of algorithms, and to remind me to live in the world of people and ukuleles, laughter and LEGO. And that was more than enough.

Chapter 1   **Algorithms**

In March of 2014, I had a memorable conversation with fellow technology-focused librarians at the closing reception of the Library Technology Conference in St. Paul, Minnesota. We discussed the social media site "This is My Jam," which I said was a great way to find new music.[1] The site allowed users to choose their favorite song of the moment and share it with others. I made a joke that we needed a similar social media site for librarians, since every librarian I knew had a favorite search that they would use whenever testing a new search tool. Mine, I explained, was "batman." As an academic librarian, this search gives me a good overview of how a search tool evaluates material types, since I expect to see popular works about the fictional superhero (mostly graphic novels and comics), movies in a variety of formats, academic texts evaluating the role of Batman in twentieth-century culture, as well as a handful of 500-year-old texts translated by Steven Batman, an English author. I said that I'd noticed several other librarians over the years using a favorite search over and over, and I found it interesting that no one ever talked about it. It wasn't something I was taught in library school, and no mentor or other librarian had suggested it to me or to the others who embraced the practice. Yet nearly everyone I spoke with had a favorite search. My fellow librarians in St. Paul all shared their favorite searches, from "Space law" to "dog and pony show." Each had come to their search on their own, with no outside encouragement, and each

---

1   A year later, the This is My Jam website shut down. As of January 2019, you can still see an archive at https://thisismyjam.com.

had well-thought out reasons for using the terms they did and the criteria for evaluating the results. Later that evening at the hotel bar with Librarian Cynthia Ng, the short-lived social network for librarians, This is My Search, was born.[2]

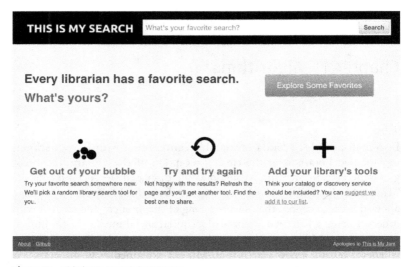

Figure 1.1   This is My Search homepage

I think often about how nearly every librarian I have met has developed, on their own, a litmus test and criteria for evaluating the dizzying array of search tools that are part of modern librarianship. In a glaring oversight of LIS education, librarians are not trained to carefully evaluate these tools, despite their ever-increasing role in our work. Part of my goal in writing this book is to not only sound the alarm regarding the magnitude of the problems we are dealing with in these library search tools, but also to arm the profession with the kinds of strategic tools and techniques for evaluating search tools and holding commercial software vendors accountable for their effectiveness. The increasing role of search in our everyday lives and our

---

2   This is My Search, the website, was shut down in 2016 due to inactivity. The code for the site is available on my Github page: https://github.com/mreidsma/thisismysearch.

academic institutions requires a more formal program of evaluation than typing catchy keywords into a few different systems and eyeballing the results to look for similarities across these varied tools. But for quite a while after my conversation in Minnesota, I continued to evaluate my tools with a single search term based on the favorite comic book of my youth. It was a year-and-a-half later before I started to see the potential impacts of ineffective search tools, although this also started with a fellow librarian's favorite search.

By the Fall of 2015, Grand Valley State University (GVSU), where I am the Web Services Librarian, had been using Ex Libris' discovery tool Summon for seven years.[3] We were their first customer, and I had served on the advisory team for the development of Summon 2.0 from 2012 until 2013. One afternoon, my colleague Jeffrey Daniels showed me the Summon results page for his go-to search, "stress in the workplace." Jeffrey likes this search because it shows how well a search tool handles word proximities, or the distance between all of the search terms in a returned result. Since Summon's index contains the full-text of many of the eBooks in GVSU's collection[4], this is a necessary feature. Since "stress" is a common term in both the social sciences and engineering, Jeffrey uses this search to see if any civil engineering books sneak into his results set, or whether the search tool's algorithm correctly looks for results that have the words "stress" and "workplace" close together. And in this case, the regular results that Summon was showing him were impressive; there were no books on bridge design. But the result for an auxiliary algorithm called the Topic Explorer had a problematic result.

The Topic Explorer is a contextual panel in the Summon results screen that helps users "display details about the search topic, helping guide

---

3   Summon was introduced by Serials Solutions, a division of ProQuest, in 2009. The Serials Solutions name was retired in 2014 in favor of ProQuest, around the time Summon 2.0 was released. The following year, ProQuest acquired their competitor, Ex Libris, and subsequently put all technology platforms under the Ex Libris portfolio, keeping the content platforms under the ProQuest name. At times you may see Summon called a Serials Solutions product, a ProQuest product, or an Ex Libris product. I will primarily refer to it as an Ex Libris product, since at the time I am writing this book in 2018 and early 2019, Summon fell under the Ex Libris name.

4   In Fall 2015, GVSU had just over one million eBooks in our catalog, although not all were in the Summon index.

the user through the research process."[5] The Topic Explorer is very similar to Google's Knowledge Graph, which aims to "better understand your query, so [Google] can summarize relevant content around that topic, including key facts you're likely to need for that particular thing."[6] The idea is that broad searches might indicate that the researcher isn't familiar with the topic they are searching for. The Topic Explorer (and Knowledge Graph) will show them contextual information, like an encyclopedia entry, related topics, and subject librarians that can help them with their research. In Jeffrey's search, the Topic Explorer had brought up a reference article from Wikipedia to help the user better understand the topic. But instead of focusing on Jeffrey's topic, "stress in the workplace", Summon returned the Wikipedia article for "Women in the workforce" (Figure 1.2). The Topic Explorer only returns a single result, and the message it sends through this design choice is that the result that is shown is *exactly* what you are searching for. But Jeffrey searched for stress, not women, and so the juxtaposition between his search terms and the result they provided made it seem like Summon (and by extension, the GVSU library[7]) was saying that stress in the workplace was really about women in the workforce. This was not a correlation we were happy to endorse.

We reported the issue to Ex Libris and they immediately blocked the Topic Explorer result for this search. It's important to note that they blocked the result—they did not investigate why their Topic Explorer algorithm made a connection between these two topics. They treated the correlation between stress and women as an isolated technical issue. But I suspected that an algorithm that would make a connection between stress and women in the workplace might also make other incorrect and biased correlations. And because Ex Libris chose not to pursue the issue further, I decided to look more closely at the Topic Explorer to better understand the

---

5   "Summon: Topic Explorer," *Summon: Product Documentation,* August 25, 2016, https://knowledge.exlibrisgroup.com/Summon/Product_Documentation/Searching_in_The_Summon_Service/Search_Results/Summon%3A_Topic_Explorer.

6   "Introducing the Knowledge Graph: Things, Not Strings," *Google Blog,* May 16, 2012, https://googleblog.blogspot.com/2012/05/introducing-knowledge-graph-things-not.html.

7   In our usability tests and other user research tests at GVSU Libraries, it was clear that many of our libraries' users are not aware that almost all of our library software is created by third-party commercial vendors.

Figure 1.2 Ex Libris' Summon search showing Stress in the workplace related to working women

workings of the Topic Explorer algorithm. I wondered whether this really was an isolated incident, and what we could do to improve the search experience for all of our users without exposing them to the kinds of bias that had appeared in the "stress in the workplace" search.

What is an Algorithm?

As algorithms have moved into the public discourse over the past few years, it is important to define what I mean by an algorithm. There are many approaches to this definition.[8] Computer Scientists define algorithms as "a description of the method by which a task is to be accomplished."[9] That is,

---

8   See, for instance, Brent Daniel Mittelstadt et al., "The Ethics of Algorithms: Mapping the Debate," *Big Data & Society* 3, no. 2 (2016): 1–21.

9   Andrew Goffey, "Algorithm," in *Software Studies: A Lexicon,* ed. Matthew Fuller (Cambridge, MA: MIT Press, 2008), 15.

"an algorithm is just a finite sequence of steps used to solve a problem."[10] In the everyday world, algorithms are broadly interpreted to be any set of instructions to complete a task. The computer scientists Brian Christian and Tom Griffiths offer up a number of common algorithms that have nothing to do with computers:

> When you cook from a recipe, you're following an algorithm. When you knit a sweater from a pattern, you're following an algorithm. When you put a sharp edge on a piece of flint by executing a precise sequence of strikes with the end of an antler—a key step in making fine stone tools—you're following an algorithm.[11]

But these basic definitions of algorithms bear little to no resemblance to the algorithms that we encounter on websites, computers, smartphones, and other devices in our everyday lives. Following a recipe to cook a meal seems an order of magnitude different from Facebook's algorithms choosing what stories will appear on a user's News Feed, or Google's search algorithms returning a few million search results in a fraction of a second. Part of this is because, for computer scientists, algorithms are "a mathematical construct."[12] A recipe is not an algorithm in computer science. According to Nick Seaver, Assistant Professor of Anthropology at Tufts University, that is because "algorithms *per se* are supposed to be strictly rational concerns, marrying the certainties of mathematics with the objectivity of technology."[13] But even this definition seems to be missing some crucial information. How are we to understand Google's search algorithms or Face-Book's News Feed algorithms as a series of mathematical steps? Our everyday understanding of algorithms is fairly far removed from "the certainties of mathematics," although technology companies have certainly worked

---

10 Brian Christian and Tom Griffiths, *Algorithms to Live By: The Computer Science of Human Decisions* (New York: Henry Holt, 2017), 3.

11 Christian and Griffiths, *Algorithms to Live By*, 4.

12 Mittelstadt et al., "The Ethics of Algorithms," 2.

13 Nick Seaver, "Knowing Algorithms," *Media in Transition* 8 (2013): 2, http://nickseaver.net/papers/seaverMiT8.pdf.

hard to instill the idea of these technical artifacts' inherent mathematical objectivity, as I will discuss in Chapter 2.

So why is there a disconnect between computer science and popular discourse around algorithms? Largely, computer science as a field hasn't moved on from thinking about algorithms in the way they have been understood for decades, even as algorithms and the idea of algorithms spread into popular use. Even within Computer Science 101 courses, there is no doubt that students have a hard time making the connection between the sample "Hello world" algorithms that their textbooks use to describe these "finite series of steps" and the complexities that they see in the world. Everyday algorithms, like Google's search algorithms, Twitter's Trending Topics, and Facebook's News Feed are actually collections of many algorithms connected together.

Other disciplines in the academy, as well as the popular press, have evolved their understanding to account for the kinds of complexities we see in algorithms in our daily lives. Rob Kitchin, a Professor at the National University of Ireland Maynooth, notes that "what constitutes an algorithm has changed over time and they can be thought of in a number of ways: technically, computationally, mathematically, politically, culturally, economically, contextually, materially, philosophically, ethically and so on."[14] This is one of the challenges in talking about algorithms: everyone may use the same term—algorithm—but the computer scientist will approach the topic technically, while the ethicist will see it ethically. Each will approach the topic from a different perspective.

For those of us who are interacting with algorithms while living our lives, we will understand algorithms differently still, if we even know we are interacting with them at all. Computer technology, powered largely by algorithmic processes, has moved into nearly every aspect of our daily lives. Nearly everything today is powered in part by algorithms: the fitness trackers we wear to track our movements, our smartphones and their voice assistants and GPS, and all of our must-have apps. Algorithms choose what we see when we search, they choose which of our friends' messages we see, and they recommend our next round of entertainment. They determine how likely we are to default on a loan, what interest rates we deserve, and

---

14 Rob Kitchin, "Thinking Critically About and Researching Algorithms," *Information, Communication & Society* 20, no. 1 (2017): 16.

whether our résumés indicate that we will be a good fit for a job. They have become so pervasive that the author and urbanist Adam Greenfield refers to their ascendancy as "the colonization of everyday life by information technology."[15]

This "colonization" is so thorough that most of us aren't even aware we are interacting with algorithms, and are surprised when it is revealed to us. Facebook made headlines over their notorious "emotional contagion" experiment, where Facebook engineers manipulated the frequency of positive and negative posts a user would see in thousands of timelines to determine whether "emotions expressed by others on Facebook influence our own emotions, constituting experimental evidence for massive-scale contagion via social networks."[16] It was news to many users that Facebook tinkered with the News Feed at all. As recently as 2013, when University of Illinois Computer Science Professor Karrie Karahalios studied Facebook's users, 62 percent of the users in her study did not realize that Facebook used algorithms to decide which news stories would appear in the News Feed.[17] (Most assumed they were seeing everything that was posted by everyone they followed.)

Many Netflix users are aware that the company uses some sort of technique to build its recommendation lists, but it also uses algorithms to determine what kinds of new content to produce, according to an interview with two content directors in the *New York Times*. Rather than planning content based on a producer or content-creator's expertise, Netflix embraces an "abiding faith in the algorithm [to] disrupt the stale conventions of an industry."[18] Local, state, and federal governments have begun using

---

15   Adam Greenfield, *Radical Technologies: The Design of Everyday Life* (London: Verso, 2017), 286.

16   Adam D.I. Kramer, Jamie E. Guillory, and Jeffrey T. Hancock, "Emotional Contagion Through Social Networks," *Proceedings of the National Academy of Sciences* 111, no. 24 (2014): 8788.

17   Karrie Karahalios, "Algorithm Awareness: How the News Feed on Facebook Decides What You Get to See," *MIT Technology Review*, October 21, 2014, https://www.technologyreview.com/s/531676/algorithm-awareness/.

18   Jason Zinoman, "The Netflix Executives Who Bent Comedy to Their Will," *New York Times*, September 10, 2018, https://www.nytimes.com/2018/09/09/arts/television/netflix-comedy-strategy-exclusive.html.

algorithms to optimize publics services, too. "Algorithms can decide where kids go to school, how often garbage is picked up, which police precincts get the most officers, where building code inspections should be targeted, and even what metrics are used to rate a teacher."[19] The reporter Julia Angwin has shown that algorithms are central to many state's criminal justice systems, often offloading the risk assessments for recidivism in sentencing to proprietary algorithms. Her research has shown that these algorithms are wrong 40 percent of the time, and are twice as likely to score blacks as being at a high risk of recidivism than whites.[20]

In her examination of algorithmic thinking gone awry, the data scientist Cathy O'Neil examined how entry-level job applications now often use a "personality test" component that is scored by an algorithm.[21] If your answers to questions about your mental health don't satisfy the algorithm, you won't be offered an interview, let alone a job. Recently, a start-up called HireVue has used algorithms to parse video recordings of job applicants to "compare a candidate's word choice, tone, and facial movements with the body language and vocabularies of their best hires."[22] Princeton University Assistant Professor Arvind Narayanan called it "an example of AI [artificial intelligence] whose only conceivable purpose is to perpetuate societal biases."[23] Countless part-time workers at chain stores like Starbucks and Walmart are scheduled by an algorithm, which is programmed to increase efficiency at the expense of any normalcy in the employees lives and schedules, making finding regular child care or making plans a week in advance

19   Jim Dwyer, "A Push to Expose the Computing Process in City Decision-Making," *New York Times,* August 24, 2017, https://www.nytimes.com/2017/08/24/nyregion/showing-the-algorithms-behind-new-york-city-services.html.

20   Julia Angwin et al., "Machine Bias: There's Software Used Across the Country to Predict Future Criminals. And It's Biased Against Blacks," *Propublica,* May 23, 2016, https://www.propublica.org/article/machine-bias-risk-assessments-in-criminal-sentencing.

21   Cathy O'Neil, *Weapons of Math Destruction: How Big Data Increases Inequality and Threatens Democracy* (New York: Crown, 2016), 105–11.

22   Monica Torres, "New App Scans Your Face and Tells Companies Whether You're Worth Hiring," *Ladders,* August 25, 2017, https://www.theladders.com/career-advice/ai-screen-candidates-hirevue.

23   Arvind Narayanan, Twitter Post, August 27, 2017, 9:57am, https://twitter.com/random_walker/status/901851127624458240

nearly impossible.[24] In her study of the algorithms that are taking over public assistance, Virginia Eubanks, Associate Professor of Political Science at SUNY Albany, shows how all of the complexity involved in traditionally helping the poor and homeless is being handed over to computer systems that aim to predict the success of these interventions with individuals.[25] She tells of an intake screener who, despite her experience and expertise, defers to an algorithm if her assessment varies from that of the machine.[26] The role of the algorithm here has become like an oracle. Writing about the takeover of public services by algorithms in *The New Yorker*, Jill Lepore, the David Woods Kemper '41 Professor of American History at Harvard University, notes that "the noble dream here is that, if only child-protective agencies collected better data and used better algorithms, children would no longer be beaten or killed."[27]

One recent moment that publicly exposed the reach of algorithms was in the spring of 2017 when Dr. David Dao was bruised and bloodied as security officers dragged him off a United Airlines flight after an algorithm determined that he was the "lowest value customer" on the overbooked flight.[28] The algorithm could only deal in quantifiable, measurable things, and so it looked for someone flying alone in coach who wasn't a rewards member and who had paid less for their ticket than others. It did not factor into the equation the reasons that Dr. Dao was traveling, or his thoughts on whether he wanted to be bumped (or the concerns of any of the other passengers, for that matter). These are not quantifiable things, and so the algorithm had not been trained to consider them. This was the moment when many of us realized the effects that algorithms can have in the real world for all of us, as we saw images of Dao's bloodied face recorded

---

24   O'Neil, *Weapons of Math Destruction*, 123–30.

25   Virginia Eubanks, *Automating Inequality: How High-Tech Tools Profile, Police, and Punish the Poor*, (New York: St. Martin's Press, 2017).

26   Eubanks, 142.

27   Jill Lepore, "Baby Doe: A Political History of Tragedy," *The New Yorker*, February 1, 2016, 56.

28   Cathy O'Neil, "United Airlines Exposes Our Twisted Idea of Dignity," *Bloomberg*, April 18, 2017, https://www.bloomberg.com/opinion/articles/2017-04-18/united-airlines-exposes-our-twisted-idea-of-dignity.

by fellow passengers. The algorithm didn't beat Dr. Dao, but United Airlines put so much faith in it that its employees resorted to violence to carry out its decision.

The reason for this disconnect between the technical logic of the algorithm and the messiness of everyday life is that the creators of algorithms believe that everything can be reduced to mathematical logic. In his account of the rise of Big Data, *New York Times* reporter Steve Lohr interviews Jeffrey Hammerbacher, co-founder of Cloudera and the man who built the data science team at Facebook, on his views about data and algorithms. Hammerbacher said that he "view[s] math as the true arena in which human intellect is demonstrated at the highest level."[29] This is not an unusual view. Lohr also talked with Virginia Rometty, the CEO of IBM, who said, "I've always believed that most solutions can be found in the roots of math."[30] But how do you write an equation that allows a person to retain their dignity and humanity when you are trying to calculate the "lowest value customer"? Because for all its power, some things cannot be readily translated into equations without over-simplification.

Algorithms and Models

Let's take a look at a few different aspects of algorithms, and assess how we can approach algorithms for the purposes of this study. First, an algorithm as a technical artifact is essentially mathematical. The trouble here is that in order for an algorithm to work, all of its inputs have to be reduced to mathematics. This doesn't necessarily mean that an algorithm only does sums, or multiplication, or complex factoring; rather, any input that isn't already quantifiable, like a Google search for the nearest coffee shop, will need to be translated into math. In this example, Google might look at the terms "coffee" and "shop," and look for results in its index where these two words are close together. But this idea of "close" will be reduced to mathematics: say, the words must be within 15 words of each other. From those results, the word "nearby" will likely be used to look through the results with

---

29   Steve Lohr, *Data-Ism: The Revolution Transforming Decision Making, Consumer Behavior, and Almost Everything Else* (New York: Harper Business, 2015), 14.

30   Lohr, 42.

geographic coordinates within a specified distance, say 10 miles, from the location of the user (as determined by IP address or phone location data). Even though this process feels like a qualitative one, in order for the algorithm to act it must be translated into a mathematical set of decisions.

In the process of translating all of our various qualitative inputs into quantitative data to be processed, algorithms "take a complex system from the world and abstract it into processes that capture some of that system's logic and discard others."[31] In the coffee shop example above, the algorithm doesn't need to know about many of the details that humans might consider when looking for a coffee shop, because they aren't actually relevant to the task: traffic and the view on the way to coffee shop, parking possibilities (or pedestrian paths), the shop's atmosphere, the flavor of the coffee, price per cup, and more. The algorithm doesn't need to worry about these criteria just to answer the very specific query for "nearby coffee shop." (It is worth noting that the algorithm could be instructed to care about these and other factors, but it must be told to do so either explicitly in the search or through programming by its creator. In the case of machine-learning algorithms, the algorithm must be given a data set that has these relevant data points available for it to analyze for patterns.)

This simplification process is called modeling, where a designer or developer creates a simulated model of some real-world phenomena in order to allow computer code (and algorithms) to complete some task. These models are largely constructed on what we already know about the task, and what is mathemetcially relevant to completing the task. Anything that isn't relevant or isn't already recorded or measurable is ignored in a model. And anything put into the model must be done in such a way that the computer understands. As Robert Boguslaw noted nearly 50 years ago, for computers to understand the world, "the world of reality must at some point in time be reduced to binary form."[32] This means that the model won't look exactly like reality, because some things have been intentionally left out and others

---

31 Ian Bogost, "The Cathedral of Computation," *The Atlantic,* January 15, 2015, https://www.theatlantic.com/technology/archive/2015/01/the-cathedral-of-computation/384300/.

32 Robert Boguslaw, "Systems of power and the power of systems," ed. Alan F. Westin, *Information Technology in a democracy* (Cambridge, MA: Harvard University Press, 1971), 425.

have been translated into a mathematical proxy that the computer can deal with. A concept that is difficult to quantify like "popularity", for instance, often is calculated by the number of likes a post has, or the number of page views, or some other quantifiable measure. Lohr summarized modeling well when he said "a model is the equivalent of a metaphor, an explanatory simplification. It usefully distills, but it also somewhat distorts."[33] But models don't just represent the world exactly as it is right now; rather, they help predict what is about to come.

As O'Neil put it, "mathematical models, by their nature, are based on the past, and on the assumption that patterns will repeat."[34] A model is made up of information relevant to the task that needs to be completed, and all "irrelevant" information is ignored or discarded. Lohr called models "tool[s] for modeling what-if decisions" with the goal of making "more accurate predictions and better decisions."[35] For the location search in our example, the model likely has geospatial coordinates of existing businesses (but not businesses that may have just opened, or filed incomplete metadata, or that do not have a digital footprint that Google can access); details about the traffic patterns in the area that were in effect when Google sent it's Street View cars out (although this data may not reflect the current state of the roads, as we'll see in a moment); and local traffic laws that were in effect when the model was created. But not all historical data applies, only that relevant to the model. Google's mapping model likely does not include information about sidewalk conditions or the location of mulberry trees, because the model's creators did not think that was relevant information in finding a route to a particular location.[36]

But incorrect and outdated information in models are not the only issues we have to deal with when creating models. The choices that the model's creators make are also important. Why are some factors important but others ignored? Often these decisions are based on assumptions of what is important. O'Neil points out how integral these choices are to the entire

---

33 Lohr, *Data-ism*, 160.

34 O'Neil, *Weapons of Math Destruction*, 38.

35 Lohr, *Data-ism*, 63.

36 As a pedestrian, during certain times of the year I will choose routes based precisely on the absence of mulberry trees or the buckling of sidewalks.

model itself, as important as the data. "Models," she says, "are constructed not just from data but from the choices we make about which data to pay attention to—and which to leave out. Those choices are not just about logistics, profits, and efficiency. They are fundamentally moral."[37] Because these choices affect the options that people have—about what information they have access to, about where they are given directions to go—there is an ethical element in the modeling process that must not be overlooked. We'll see more about how this plays out in search algorithms' claims to objectivity in Chapter 2.

Black Boxes

Of course, I don't actually know specifically how Google handles answering queries. I'm working off an understanding of how search tools are built, but the reality of Google's search algorithm is no doubt several orders of magnitude more complex than my example. We do know a few of the things Google takes into account, like how many other sites link to a page, "how often and where the keywords being searched for show up on a specific page, how recently the page was created (a sign of the freshness of the information) and the location of the person making the search."[38] I also don't have access to the model of the world that Google has created to simplify the process of designing their tools. Commercial algorithms are "black boxes," a term with a long history in the study of cybernetics to mean a system whose workings are hidden from view. These search algorithms are black boxes "in that they produce material effects in the world without necessarily revealing anything about how they did so."[39] Search algorithms are largely kept secret because they are the primary intellectual property asset of the parent company, and so sharing the details of how they work would devalue the primary revenue-generating asset the company has.

---

37   O'Neil, *Weapons of Math Destruction*, 218.

38   Daisuke Wakabayashi, "Trump Says Google Is Rigged, Despite Its Denials. What Do We Know About How It Works?," *New York Times,* September 5, 2018, https://www.nytimes.com/2018/09/05/technology/google-trump-bias.html.

39   Greenfield, *Radical Technologies,* 244.

In an interview with the *New York Times,* author and technologist Jaron Lanier noted how the "black box" nature of much of the commercial internet isn't how it was supposed to be.

> "The whole internet thing was supposed to create the world's best information resource in all of history," [Lanier] says. "Everything would be made visible. And instead we're living in this time of total opacity where you don't know why you see the news you see. You don't know if it's the same news that someone else sees. You don't know who made it that way, You don't know who's paid to change what you see. Everything is totally obscure in a profound way that it never was before."[40]

But one of the reasons companies are touting the benefits of algorithms is for precisely the opposite reason: they claim that computers are somehow more transparent than the decision-making process of humans. Eubanks finds this

> philosophy that sees human beings as unknowable black boxes and machines as transparent deeply troubling. It seems to me a worldview that surrenders any attempt at empathy and forecloses the possibility of ethical developments. The presumption that human decision-making is opaque and inaccessible is an admission that we have abandoned a social commitment to try to understand each other.[41]

Perhaps the advocates of algorithms feel that they can understand how their algorithms work, even if the inner workings are kept from the public. But Zenyep Tufakci, an Associate Professor at the School of Information and Library Science at the University of North Carolina, Chapel Hill, notes that "programmers do not, and often cannot, predict what their complex programs will do."[42] Her point is that algorithms are more than just

---

40   Maureen Dowd, "Soothsayer in the Hills Sees Silicon Valley's Sinister Side," *New York Times,* November 8, 2017, https://www.nytimes.com/2017/11/08/style/jaron-lanier-new-memoir.html.

41   Eubanks, *Automating Inequality,* 168.

42   Zeynep Tufekci, "The real bias built in at Facebook," *New York Times,* May 19, 2016, https://www.nytimes.com/2016/05/19/opinion/the-real-bias-built-in-at-facebook.html.

assemblages of code, that they cannot be examined without seeing them in context with the data they use and the effects they create.

The Social Aspects of Algorithms

So far our discussion of algorithms has been limited to the technical, mathematical artifact created by software developers. But this view is limiting, in that algorithms are designed to do something, and to interact with the world. "We can only understand what technologies really do, and how they really work, when we are able to stand back and weigh their consequences for all the social and natural ecosystems into which they are knit."[43]

But the definition of an "algorithm" we've been discussing still retains the tension between the popular definition of the term and the specific definition common to computer science. The key to finding a way to resolve this tension is to bring the algorithm out of the abstract and into the world in which it works.

Malte Ziewitz, Assistant Professor and Mills Family Faculty Fellow in the Department of Science and Technology Studies at Cornell University, notes that in the popular press,

> algorithms have developed into somewhat of a modern myth. On the one hand, they have been depicted as powerful entities that rule, sort, govern, shape, or otherwise control our lives. On the other hand, their alleged obscurity and inscrutability make it difficult to understand what exactly is at stake.[44]

Paul Dourish, the Chancellor's Professor of Informatics and Associate Dean for Research in the Donald Bren School of Information and Computer Sciences at the University of California, Irvine, emphasizes that "the limits of the term algorithm are determined by social engagements rather than by

---

43   Greenfield, *Radical Technologies*, 298.

44   Malte Ziewitz, "Governing Algorithms: Myth, Mess, and Methods," *Science, Technology, & Human Values* 41, no. 1 (2016): 3.

technological or material constraints."[45] That is, what constitutes an algorithm has changed throughout time because of the varied social role that algorithms have played.

And even my term "popular understanding" may be misleading, according to the fieldwork Seaver has conducted. In his interviews with employees of a technology company, even those tasked with literally writing the code that executes the service's algorithms, the term "'algorithm' had a vague, 'non-technical' meaning, indicating various properties of a broader 'algorithmic system', even in nominally 'technical' settings."[46] So even those practitioners of computer science, whose definition is the tightest and most technical seem to talk about algorithms in a more fuzzy, "systems" focused way in practice. It would seem that the key to resolving this understanding of what we mean by an algorithm is in bringing these technical and social understandings together.

We must be careful not to simply place our technical understanding of the algorithm in a social context. As Seaver notes, we must understand algorithms "not as stable objects interacted with from many perspectives, but as the manifold consequences of a variety of human practices."[47] That is, the algorithm is never a fixed thing, for many reasons. First and foremost, the technical aspect of an algorithm is always changing, with software developers making tweaks and adjustments to improve its performance. At any given time, there are hundreds of experiments going on with large algorithms such as Google Search, Facebook's News Feed, or other algorithmically-driven tools, making the identification of "the algorithm" tricky. If your search uses a different version of the algorithm from mine, despite searching for the same keywords at the same time, did we use the same algorithm?

What's more, because so much of what these algorithms hope to act upon must be "translated" into mathematical form, no two developers may make the same analysis on how exactly to make some difficult-to-measure attribute fit into a mathematical formula. To assume that concepts like

---

45 Paul Dourish, "Algorithms and Their Others: Algorithmic Culture in Context," *Big Data & Society* 3, no. 2 (2016): 3.

46 Nick Seaver, "Algorithms as Culture: Some Tactics for the Ethnography of Algorithmic Systems," *Big Data & Society* 4, no. 2 (2017): 3.

47 Seaver, 4.

"popularity" or "affinity" (to use one of Facebook's favorite attributes) can be easily quantified "is to miss the amount of interpretive, cultural work required to translate these features into computable form. It is to mistake maps for territories."[48] Understanding the decisions and cultures of the organizations that create these algorithms is as important as understanding the code itself. The "algorithm" is ever evolving, ever changing, and the reasoning behind its decisions and choices, from the business goals that drive the product managers to the worldviews of the individual engineers who write the code help to better contextualize the actual workings of the algorithm. The only constant in all this is that the algorithms themselves, as well as the teams that make them, are ever evolving. Calling back to Hereclitus' famous aphorism, Seaver quips, "you can't log into the same Facebook twice."[49]

But the evolving technical nature of the algorithm isn't the only aspect that needs to be understood as causing flux. As Kitchin says, "algorithms need to be recognized as being ontogenetic, performative and contingent: that is, they are never fixed in nature, but are emergent and constantly unfolding."[50] Because algorithms themselves are designed to act upon data from the world and produce results, they change the way we interact with the world. And because these algorithms are iteratively developed based on how users interact with them, developers change the algorithms to adapt to the changes the algorithms have caused in our behavior. The algorithm and the user co-evolve together. Greenfield, paraphrasing Churchill's famous line, said "now we make networks, and they shape us every bit as much as any building ever did, or could."[51]

So how do we refer to this "algorithm" that is more than just instructions, more than just code, more than a technical artifact, something that also includes the data it works on, the people who create it and use it, the social feedback loop that helps us co-evolve with it, and countless other pieces that are "knit" into the fabric of our world, to use Greenfield's phrase?[52] Seaver proposes that "it is not the algorithm, narrowly defined [in

---

48 Seaver, "Knowing Algorithms," 9.

49 Seaver, 6.

50 Kitchin, "Thinking critically about and researching algorithms," 21.

51 Greenfield, *Radical Technologies,* 28.

52 Greenfield, 298.

a technical sense], that has sociocultural effects, but algorithmic systems—intricate, dynamic arrangements of people and code."[53] These "algorithmic systems" must be understood together, because without the social context of use, the algorithm is nothing more than a technical artifact. We cannot understand what it "does" as lines of code any more than the developers who wrote it. Without the data that it will act upon, we cannot begin to see how inputs will become outputs. But all of this is still experimenting on technology. The real place for understanding the algorithm is in practice, not merely in how it works technically, but how it continues to unfold in our lives as we use it, how it changes us and we change it.

There are obvious questions to ask about the technical artifact and how it creates particular outputs. For instance, how did Ex Libris' Summon discovery system make a connection between "stress in the workplace" and "women in the workforce," as in Figure 1.2? Or when, in 2015, Google Photos automatically labeled photographs of two black friends as "gorillas?"[54] How did the Google Photos algorithm make that particular association, one that dredged up hundreds of years of institutionalized racism?

But these are technical questions and their answers are merely technical—they will not begin to address the impact that the algorithm has on the individuals who use them, or society as a whole. For instance, Brent Cook, the Summon Project Manager at Ex Libris, pointed to a technical glitch in their algorithm that he called a "Mad Libs" effect, something that would match a phrase and allow you to replace one word and keep the rest of the phrase intact. Instead of typing "stress in the workplace," you could also type "heroes in the workplace," and still get a response of "women in the workplace."[55] This answer was given to try to neutralize the effects of the result that appeared biased against women, because you could also make it biased *for* women! But the problem with this approach is that Ex Libris focused solely on the technical aspects of the problem. They didn't address what happens when young women, amidst a culture that devalues their contributions in the workplace both culturally and monetarily, see working

53   Seaver, "Knowing Algorithms," 9.

54   "Google apologises for Photos app's racist blunder," *BBC News,* July 1, 2015, https://www.bbc.com/news/technology-33347866.

55   Brent Cook (Summon Project Manager, Ex Libris), email message to author, February 1, 2016.

women equated with stress in the workplace in a supposedly objective, neutral tool that everyone at the their University tells them will give them the most appropriate, scholarly information.

In the case of Google Photos, an engineer admitted that the "problem" with the autotagging was that the training set of photographs they used to "teach" Google Photos to identify the subjects of photos had very few black faces, and so it didn't know how to identify one.[56] This is also a technical explanation, but it ignores the fact that centuries of human-driven systemic racism were spouted out by an algorithmic system within hours of it launching. How does that affect the millions of black users of Google Photos, or for that matter, white supremacist users? What does it say about the engineering team that the training photos they had access to were not representative of the diversity of faces? What does it say that an algorithm that could not immediately identify a human's face immediately downgraded it to the status of an animal, the same technique that racists have used for hundreds of years?

To focus on algorithms as technical artifacts means that we will be trapped into accepting limited, technical excuses for moral lapses on the parts of these companies whose work affects hundreds of millions of people every day. We must keep the algorithmic system in our sights, always understanding that the algorithm as code acts in the world, is put in motion by a group of people who themselves are products of a particular culture in a particular time and place. And each time we interact with the algorithms, each part of the system comes back subtly changed. For Seaver, rather than being separate concerns,

> 'cultural' details *are* technical details—the tendencies of an engineering team are as significant as the tendencies of a sorting algorithm. This is not so much an attempt to add the cultural back onto the technical as it is a refusal of the cultural/technical distinction as a ground for analysis.[57]

---

56 Yonatan Zunger, Twitter Post, June 29, 2015, 11:21am, https://twitter.com/yonatanzunger/status/615585776110170112. See also Sara Wachter-Boettcher, *Technically Wrong: Sexist Apps, Biased Algorithms, and Other Threats of Toxic Tech* (New York: W.W. Norton, 2017), 133.

57 Seaver, "Knowing Algorithms," 10.

Faith and Reality

Despite the ever-evolving nature of algorithmic systems, we are firm in our faith in their ability to outperform human decision making. The examples above showing a tiny selection of where algorithms touch the lives of everyone helps to see their reach. Algorithms now help control traffic lights to optimize traffic patterns, they help decide both how much your attention is worth when you visit a web page (by auctioning off the advertising space on the page based on what it knows about you),[58] as well as how much the items you are interested in will be priced.[59] Algorithms decide what kinds of "answers" you will see to the questions you ask Google and other search engines, and what kinds of messages you will see on your social media feeds. The power we have ceded to these systems of code and culture is powerful. Frank Pasquale, Professor of Law at the University of Maryland Francis King Carey School of Law, notes that now, "authority is increasingly expressed algorithmically. Decisions that used to be based on human reflection are now made automatically."[60] One reason for this increase in algorithmic authority is our increasing faith that the algorithm will deliver a more objective decision than a human could, that somehow the algorithm eliminates the human biases that we often see coloring our decisions. In the next chapter we will examine the role that "objectivity" plays in the popular understanding of algorithms, but first it is worth reflecting for a moment on the power that our belief in that objectivity, in the supposed "rightness" of the authority wielded by computers, does to our understanding of the world and our place in it. We have already seen how our popular understanding of algorithms can be at odds with the more technical understanding. So within an algorithmic system, how do these different views play out in how we

---

58 Natasha Singer, "Your Online Attention, Bought in an Instant," *New York Times*, November 17, 2012, https://www.nytimes.com/2012/11/18/technology/your-online-attention-bought-in-an-instant-by-advertisers.html.

59 Julia Angwin and Surya Mattu, "Amazon Says It Puts Customers First. But Its Pricing Algorithm Doesn't," *ProPublica*, September 20, 2016, https://www.propublica.org/article/amazon-says-it-puts-customers-first-but-its-pricing-algorithm-doesnt.

60 Frank Pasquale, *The Black Box Society: The Secret Algorithms That Control Money and Information* (Cambridge, MA: Harvard University Press, 2015), 8.

approach the use of algorithms? And specifically, how do we approach the most trusted algorithmic systems, search engines?

According to *New York Times* writer Daisuke Wakabayashi, "online search and Google are synonymous."[61] It handles around 3.5 billion searches a day from over four billion Internet users, or nearly half the population of the world.[62] Google overall handles nearly three quarters of the online searches on desktops or laptops, and over 80% of mobile searches.[63] According to Google, 15% of the search queries it sees every day are ones it has never seen before.[64] This is quite different than the state of search engines 15 years ago, when the major three—Google, MSN, and Yahoo!—each held around 30% of the market.[65] Google and others have attributed the rise of Google to being "synonymous with search" to its superior ranking algorithms,[66] which it has described as "computer programs that look for clues to give you back exactly what you want."[67]

That kind of market dominance gives "the company an enormous role in directing the world-wide flow of information on the internet."[68] And Google agrees, arguing that users come to Google "for more than just

---

61 Wakabayashi, "Trump Says Google Is Rigged."

62 "Internet Live Stats," Internet Live Stats, accessed October 1, 2018, http://www.internetlivestats.com/.

63 "Search Engine Market Share," Net Market Share, accessed October 1, 2018, https://www.netmarketshare.com/search-engine-market-share.aspx.

64 "Useful Responses Take Many Forms," Google Search, accessed January 31, 2019, https://www.google.com/search/howsearchworks/responses/#?modal_active=none.

65 John MacCormick, *9 Algorithms That Changed the Future: The Ingenious Ideas That Drive Today's Computers* (Princeton, NJ: Princeton University Press, 2012), 11.

66 MacCormick, 11.

67 This version was quoted in Tufekci, "The real bias built in at Facebook." The marketing language around Google Search has changed in recent years, largely in response to the rise of deliberately misleading information. Google now avoids saying that it "gives you exactly what you want" and instead says it "give[s] you useful and relevant results." "How Search Works," Google Search, accessed December 11, 2018, https://www.google.com/search/howsearchworks/.

68 Wakabayashi, "Trump Says Google Is Rigged."

links—they go for information."[69] Google's page on "How Search Algorithms Work" says that "you want the answer, not a billion web pages."[70] Whenever Google mentions search results, they refer to "information" or "answers" rather than literally what the results are: links to web pages. The overall message is that Google is a search engine to be trusted, and the market dominance Google has attained shows that users believe them. Tarleton Gillespie, a Principal Researcher at Microsoft Research New England and an Affiliated Associate Professor at Cornell, emphasizes this when he writes about search engines and algorithms. He notes that they are "more than mere tools, algorithms are also stabilizers of trust, practical and symbolic assurances that their evaluations are fair and accurate, free from subjectivity, error, or attempted influence."[71] But all of this focus on being a trustworthy source of information, as well as its "Focus on the User" (which is one of three principles they list as their approach to search),[72] obscures the fact that Google is a multinational corporation whose primary responsibility is earning money for its shareholders. One reason these aspects are not highlighted, and are in fact covered over, is that they call into question the image of the objective, perfectly rational information machine, as Gillespie has pointed out.

> Search engines, while promising to provide a logical set of results in response to a query, are in fact algorithms designed to take a range of criteria into account so as to serve up results that satisfy not just the user, but the aims of the provider, their understanding of relevance or newsworthiness or public import, and the particular demands of their business model.[73]

---

69 Wakabayashi.

70 "How Search Algorithms Work," Google Search, accessed January 4, 2019, https://www.google.com/search/howsearchworks/algorithms/.

71 Tarleton Gillespie, "The Relevance of Algorithms," in *Media Technologies: Essays on communication, materiality, and society,* ed. Tarleton Gillespie, Pablo J. Boczkowski and Kirsten A. Foot (Cambridge, MA: MIT Press, 2014), 179.

72 "Our Mission," Google Search, accessed November 10, 2018, https://www.google.com/search/howsearchworks/mission/.

73 Tarleton Gillespie, "Can an algorithm be wrong?," *Limn* 1, no. 2 (2012), https://limn.it/can-an-algorithm-be-wrong/.

There is a tension here between what Google wants Google to be, and what we think Google is. As O'Neil noted, Google's "search engine algorithm appears to be focused on raising revenue. But search results, if Google so chose, could have a dramatic effect on what people learn and how they vote."[74] The one correction I would make to O'Neil is this: Google cannot *choose* whether or not to influence what its users learn by showing some results and not others, structured as a ranked list. Google *always* influences what its users learn by the very nature of its search results design. Sometimes what is learned is shaped intentionally, as in the 2016 United States Presidential Campaign, when groups working on behalf of Russia waged a misinformation campaign over Google and social media sites to influence the election. Often, however, there is no focused plan for shaping what Google's users learn, other than the logic of the search algorithm.

Google's business model is quite different from the library search engines we will be examining later in this book. But the faith we have in search engines, whether specialized search tools like library discovery systems or general-purpose search engines like Google or Bing, are beliefs we carry with us throughout all of our interactions with search. That's why it is so important to begin any examination of library search tools with an examination of our relationship with Google. Libraries and vendors advertise these discovery services as "Google for libraries," because they want to engender the same kind of authoritativeness and trust that users have with Google. But despite the overwhelming trust that we have in search engines, they are much more than we understand them to be, and this tension between our faith in search engines and the reality of these algorithms is the focal point of this study.

In addition to not understanding the role that a search engine's business model plays in shaping the information we see, there is also the matter of our faith in what exactly search engines as tools can do for us. Gillespie notes that "there is a tension between what we understand these algorithms to be, what we need them to be, and what they in fact are."[75] Our understanding of Google as an all-knowing oracle does not match up with the reality of the search engine. In fact, when we encounter a glitch in the system

---

74   O'Neil, *Weapons of Math Destruction*, 184.

75   Gillespie, "Can an algorithm be wrong?"; See also Pasquale, *The Black Box Society*, 77.

that might indicate that Google isn't perfect, we tend to blame ourselves, rather than point the finger at the search engine or the team who creates it. We've bought the story that Google has sold us, rather than evaluating the tool on its own merits. Greenfield notes that "what matters most in weighing the degree to which we surrender control to an automated decision-making process isn't so much what a system can actually do, but what we believe it can do."[76]

I have talked briefly about what we think a search algorithm can do, helped along by our own positive experiences with successful Google searches and their clever marketing team. But what can the search tool actually do? This is a question that will drive much of the rest of this book, but it is worth looking in general here at some of the guiding principles of algorithms and how they call into question many of our beliefs about their objectivity and neutrality. After all, search engines in particular, from Google to library search, wield an impressive power. Pasquale has said "the power to include, exclude, and rank is the power to ensure which public impressions become permanent and which remain fleeting."[77]

Algorithms, as we have seen, are based largely on simplifications of the real world called models. The trouble with models is that "no model can include all of the real world's complexity… Inevitably, some important information gets left out."[78] And what's more, the world is represented purely as that which can be manipulated mathematically, so activities or qualities that don't lend themselves easily to measurement are often assigned proxies that can be measured. Algorithms themselves operate on their own internal logic, prioritizing efficiency and speed over thoroughness or even correctness. Christian and Griffiths note that in algorithm design, "computation is *bad*: the underlying directive of any good algorithm is to minimize the labor of thought."[79] This means that algorithms themselves are not designed to actually sort through all available data to find the "best" or "most relevant" results (whatever those qualities might mean to the creators of the algorithm). Instead, the algorithm is designed to prioritize efficiency of

---

76   Greenfield, *Radical Technologies,* 254.

77   Pasquale, *The Black Box Society,* 61.

78   O'Neil, *Weapons of Math Destruction,* 20.

79   Christian and Griffiths, *Algorithms to Live By,* 258.

computation. This is one reason that Google highlights the speed of computing its search results. Good algorithms "are all about doing what makes the most sense in the least amount of time, which by no means involves giving careful consideration to every factor and pursuing every computation to the end."[80]

Algorithms, and in particular search algorithms, are sold to us as disinterested, objective, neutral information gathering tools that find us answers. But a closer look at algorithms shows us that corporate profit motives, the nature of computer science and mathematics, reductive models of the world, and a fetish for speed and efficiency are also factors that help shape how they are designed and how they work. But one question remains: once we put our faith in these algorithmic systems, how do they affect us? How are we changed by our interactions with them?

Algorithms Change, and Change Us

The faith we put in search algorithms to manage the information we seek and consume requires us to assess the impact this reliance has on us. Does our faith in search change the way we think? Does it change the way we see the world? The way we interact with one another? As Alex Halavais, Associate Professor of Sociology at Arizona State University, noted in his study, *Search Engine Society*, "no new technology leaves us unchanged, and often the changes are unexpected and unpredictable."[81] One reason these effects are difficult to predict and see is that the engineering mindset that we use for creating and tweaking algorithms isn't well suited for seeing algorithms in context, for examining how they interact with data and the social conditions where users find them. The philosopher Iris Murdoch has said that a human "is a creature who makes pictures of himself [sic] and then comes to resemble the picture. This is the process which moral philosophy must attempt to describe and analyze."[82] Murdoch's concept of humanity "making

---

80   Christian and Griffiths, 261.

81   Alex Halavais, *Search Engine Society* (Cambridge, UK: Polity, 2009), 30.

82   Iris Murdoch, *Existentialists and Mystics: Writings on Philosophy and Literature* (New York: Allen Lane/Penguin Press, 1997), 75.

pictures of itself" relates directly to technology, which is often created to append or improve upon some perceived deficit in our humanity. Engineers create search engines because the world's knowledge is too much for any individual to assess. And so they create an image of a person who can rely on an external system to do the sorting for them so they can act on that information. In the short span of just a decade or so, that new vision of a person has come to be for almost half the population of the earth. What are the unforseen and unintended consequences of this changing relationship between humans and information? How has this change affected us and our perception of the world?

Search engines say they are tools for revealing information to us, ranked and organized by relevance to our needs. But by their very nature, search engines and other algorithmic systems are also tools of ignoring, as much as of showing.[83] The mechanisms that determine what is shown to us at any given time are not merely a function of the result's objective usefulness to our search. Rather, these algorithms are designed to serve particular objectives, often those associated with profit generation, as we have seen. This is why YouTube's recommendation algorithms have been scrutinized over the past year for emphasizing conspiracy-theory videos and Facebook's single-minded emphasis on "engagement," which led to a promotion of deliberately false or misleading information on the platform.[84] These algorithms prioritize content that increases engagement, which can only be understood by the companies involved as measurable clicks, likes, plays, or comments. (Passively reading a post that inspires you to take action offline is not measurable by the algorithm, and therefore is not considered engagement.) Facebook and YouTube have shown themselves to be venues where a lot of algorithmically significant "engagement" happens around hateful, biased, untrue, and otherwise inflammatory content because those kinds of posts and videos generate more engagement than others. More measurable engagement by users translates into more profit for the algorithm's creators. In turn, this changes how we interact with each other off

---

83   Halavais, *Search Engine Society,* 57.

84   Steve Kovach, "YouTube and Facebook Promoted a Right-Wing Conspiracy About a Florida Shooting Survivor," *Business Insider,* February 21, 2018, https://www.businessinsider.com/youtube-promotes-conspiracy-theory-video-florida-shooting-survivor-david-hogg-2018-2?r=UK&IR=T.

these platforms. For instance, misleading, racist posts on Facebook are suspected to be the cause of mob violence and murders in India and Myanmar.[85] And the "emotional contagion" experiment at Facebook, where researchers intentionally manipulated users' offline emotional state through the content in their News Feed, shows "Facebook's enormous power to affect what we learn, how we feel, and whether we vote."[86] And even the YouTube Kids' app was found to promote videos to children advocating that the earth is "run by reptile-human hybrids" and that the moon landing never happened,[87] all in the name of "engagement." Search engines are not immune, as Associate Professor of Information Studies at UCLA Safiya Umoja Noble detailed in her book, *Algorithms of Oppression*. When Dylan Roof went to Google and typed in "black on white crime," Google recommended a series of white-supremacist websites that the future mass-murderer said helped shape his thinking on race relations, and led him to murder nine black strangers in a church in Charleston, South Carolina.[88] As Pasquale notes, "despite their claims of objectivity and neutrality, [search tools] are constantly making value-laden, controversial decisions. They help create the world they claim to merely 'show' us."[89]

---

85   Mike Isaac and Sheera Frenkel, "Facebook Security Breach Exposes Accounts of 50 Million Users," *New York Times*, September 28, 2018, https://www.nytimes.com/2018/09/28/technology/facebook-hack-data-breach.html.

86   O'Neil, *Weapons of Math Destruction*, 184. In addition to the "emotional contagion" experiment, Facebook runs thousands of experiments every year on user data. In 2010, for instance, they ran an experiment to prove that they could influence the number of people who showed up to vote, especially by using Facebook "friendships" to encourage users (Robert M. Bond et al., "A 61-Million-Person Experiment in Social Influence and Political Mobilization," *Nature* 489, no. 7415 (2012), https://www.ncbi.nlm.nih.gov/pmc/articles/PMC3834737/). Also in 2010, Facebook tracked whether the information sharing behavior of your Facebook friends affected your own information sharing habits (Eytan Bakshy et al., "The Role of Social Networks in Information Diffusion," *Proceedings of the 21st International Conference on World Wide Web* (2010), https://dl.acm.org/citation.cfm?doid=2187836.2187907).

87   James Cook, "The YouTube Kids App Has Been Suggesting a Load of Conspiracy Videos to Children," *Business Insider*, March 17, 2018, https://www.businessinsider.com/youtube-suggested-conspiracy-videos-to-children-using-its-kids-app-2018-3/?op=1.

88   Safiya Umoja Noble, *Algorithms of Oppression: How Search Engines Reinforce Racism* (New York: New York University Press, 2018), 115.

89   Pasquale, *The Black Box Society*, 61.

Search algorithms also affect how we see the world, and may be changing the way we think. Fifteen years ago the researchers Kathleen Guinee, Maya Eagleton, and Tracy E. Hall studied the search strategies of adolescent Internet users, and found four common strategies for recovering from failed searches. What they found was that the most common stratagem was "re-framing their inquiries around what can be easily found,"[90] essentially changing their way of thinking to better fit the limits of the search engine.[91] This is similar to a technique called "satisficing,"[92] where a user of a technology uses the minimum amount of effort to retrieve a usable result. These tendencies are becoming prevalent in many of our interactions with algorithmic systems, and not just search engines. Adapting to the logic of the system is most evident in voice assistants—try getting Siri or Alexa to help you with a task when you are not familiar with the way engineers assumed you would ask. After a number of responses like "I don't understand" you may give up and do the task yourself. But also accepting what the search engine provides you rather than pushing the tool to give you better results point to a disturbing trend in how we are beginning to approach our everyday interactions with information. A decade ago Halavais warned us of "the possibility that search engines encourage us to frame our thinking in terms of search."[93] And here we are.

As I write this, there is an ongoing story about whether Google biases its search results to intentionally suppress positive stories about conservative politicians in the United States.[94] Behind this story is a special sort of anxiety we have about our relationship with this technology. As Halavais puts it, "the core social question for a search engine is 'who sees what under what circumstances and in what context?' and in answering this question,

---

90   Kathleen Guinee, Maya Eagleton, and Tracy E. Hall, "Adolescents' Internet Search Strategies: Drawing Upon Familiar Cognitive Paradigms When Accessing Electronic Information Sources," *Journal of Educational Computing Research*, 29, no. 3 (2003): 370.

91   See also Halavais, *Search Engine Society*, 87.

92   Herbert A. Simon, "Rational Choice and the Structure of the Environment," *Psychological Review* 63, no. 2 (1956): 129.

93   Halavais, *Search Engine Society*, 94.

94   Daisuke Wakabayashi and Cecilia Kang, "It's Google's Turn in Washington's Glare," *New York Times*, September 26, 2018, https://www.nytimes.com/2018/09/26/technology/google-conservatives-washington.html.

political and economic battles are inevitable."[95] With the personalization of search results now commonplace, taking into account your past search history, your location, the device you are using, demographic information that the algorithm has guessed about you (which can be eerily correct about three-quarters of the time[96])—Google will show you a list of results it has calculated will be most relevant to you. It does this under the cloak of objectivity and neutrality, by emphasizing the role algorithms play in the process, and downplaying the role that humans play. But what is this objectivity based on? Can an algorithm truly be objective? And how are library search engines similar or different from Google? Are their algorithms any better? Do any of these search tools deserve the kind of blind trust we put in them?

---

95 Halavais, *Search Engine Society,* 118.

96 Michael Carl Tschantz et al., "The Accuracy of the Demographic Inferences Shown on Google's Ad Settings," *Tech. Report TR-16-003, International Computer Science Institute, 2016,* October, 2016, https://www1.icsi.berkeley.edu/~mct/pubs/wpes18/.

Chapter 2 Search Engines

To examine the algorithmic systems that make up search engines, we must first determine how search engines differ from other algorithmic systems. After all, Facebook's News Feed offers a search tool, as does Yelp, Spotify, and Amazon. Are these tools search engines?

Each of these tools has elements of a search engine within it. Facebook is the easiest to dismiss, since it's main purpose is to get users to look at the algorithms that make up the News Feed, so that their advertising algorithms can precisely target advertisements based on a dizzyingly detailed profile for each of its more than a billion users. Facebook's search is merely an add-on. Yelp and Amazon are different—both have search at their core. After all, if you want to find a restaurant near you, you use Yelp's search feature to find it. (Or, increasingly, you use Google to search and Google shows you Yelp's results.) Amazon, too, relies on search to allow shoppers to find the items they are looking for (and then recommends similar items through other parts of its algorithmic system). But Yelp and Amazon do have limits to what they search: you cannot find answers to questions about cooking a curry from scratch on Yelp (unless you find a curry restaurant and ask the chef to teach you). Likewise, you cannot find these answers on Amazon (unless you purchase a book on cooking curry). Yelp has a specialized search tool for searching reviews, while Amazon's search helps you find products to buy. Neither is a general purpose search tool like Google, where you find information on cooking curry, find good deals on products, see reviews, and more. Google can help you find your dream job, prepare for the interview, and learn to negotiate a salary. You can use the Google search box to do arithmetic, define words, and ask for the current time in any location (See Figure 2.1). It can show you factual information, or lies and deception. It can show you information that challenges your beliefs, or reinforces biases and stereotypes you might not know you have. People can (and do) go to Google with any and all questions they may have. This is why John Battelle, one of the cofounders of *WIRED*, called Google a "database of intentions."[1]

Figure 2.1   The many hidden functions of Google

We can break down the work of a general purpose search engine into two phases: first, the search tool *matches* items in its index with the search terms. Items that have the exact keyword or similar keywords will be returned as search results. Depending on the tool, it might have different criteria for what items it will return. If multiple keywords are used, the tool may prioritize results with all of those keywords present before an item will be returned. (This is the default behavior of most general purpose search engines, which inserts a boolean AND between all keywords in a search.) Some search tools that index the full text of websites or books may only return results if all of the keywords appear within the same paragraph, or within a few sentences of each other. What is common among all search engines is that they won't return results that don't have any matches to your search keywords.

Greenfield identifies three measures for evaluating the matching ability of a search algorithm. First, is *accuracy*, which is measured by seeing

---

1   John Battelle, "The Database of Intentions," *John Battelle's Search Blog*, November 13 2003, https://battellemedia.com/archives/2003/11/the_database_of_intentions.

whether all items that are returned actually match the search terms. This differs from *precision,* which is the measure of whether all the items that are known to match the search terms were identified. And finally, *recall* is a measure of whether a complete set of results is returned.[2] High accuracy in a matching algorithm means that there will be no false positives in the set. All of the items returned will match the search criteria. Low recall means that there will be many false negatives, where plenty of results that should be returned were not.

The second stage in any search is *ranking* the results that were matched. This is where search engines really tend to differ. Fifteen years ago, Google, Yahoo!, and MSN each shared about 30% of the market.[3] It is generally assumed that Google has achieved its current market dominance (nearly 80% of all searches in late 2018, according to Net Market Share)[4] through its efforts at making a ranking algorithm that users found to be better than the competition.[5]

According to Dickinson College Associate Professor of Computer Science John MacCormick, most search engines combine their matching and their ranking into a single process in order to return results as quickly as users expect.[6] Even if items are matched and ranked within a single computational process, the processes themselves are conceptually different. You must first have a matched item before you can rank it. But we don't know enough about how these proprietary algorithms are created to fully understand how they integrate these two processes. And frankly, this isn't an interesting question. The more interesting question is not how they structure code to rank and match, but how search engines decide to rank their results.

Many search tools allow you to determine how you want to rank the results of your search. On Amazon, for instance, you can choose to rank results by price (highest to lowest, or lowest to highest); by popularity (highest customer reviews first); or by recency (newest arrivals first). These

---

2 Greenfield, *Radical Technologies,* 217.

3 MacCormick, *9 Algorithms That Changed the Future,* 11.

4 Net Market Share, "Search Engine Market Share."

5 Wakabayashi, "Trump Says Google Is Rigged, Despite Its Denials."

6 MacCormick, *9 Algorithms That Changed the Future,* 11.

particular ranking mechanisms are understandable by most users. By sorting by price, we expect to see the results at the top be either higher or lower than the one after it, depending on which we choose. We would not expect to see items with low customer reviews at the top of the results if we chose to sort by popularity. By default, however, your results are listed by "relevance." There are no public-facing help documents for Amazon that explain the sorting feature, so by looking in the developer documentation we can see that when we sort by relevance, ranking will:

> Order items by keywords. Rank is determined by the keywords in the product description, if there are multiple keywords, how closely they occur in descriptions, and how often customers purchased items they found using the keyword. Keyword placement is also important. For example, the rank is higher when keywords are in titles.[7]

Note here that Amazon tells us a few of the things it takes into account when ranking items, but probably not everything. It also doesn't tell us how each of these criteria are weighted. It says that "the rank is higher when keywords are in titles," but not how it determines how much higher to rank items with keywords in the title. Google doesn't allow you to change the ranking of its search results at all, which makes understanding how Google ranks matched results even more opaque.

Ranking is complex and poorly understood, since the ranking algorithms of Google and other search engines are considered proprietary, secret information. But they have significant effects on the users of the search tools. The researchers Yvonne Kammerer and Peter Gerjets ran a study in 2012 that showed that most search results pages didn't give users enough information to evaluate whether the results they saw useful to them, so they instead "rely on superficial, but prominent, cues such as the ranking position" to help them find their results.[8] But there is more that affects

---

7   "Sort by Popularity, Price, or Condition," Amazon Web Services, accessed October 10, 2018, https://docs.aws.amazon.com/AWSECommerceService/latest/DG/SortingbyPopularityPriceorCondition.html.

8   Yvonne Kammerer and Peter Gerjets, "How Search Engine Users Evaulate and Select Web Search Results: The Impact of Seach Engine Interface on Credibility Assessments," in *Web Search Engine Research,* ed. Dirk Lewandowski (Emerald Publishing Limited, 2012), 261.

users' interpretation of search results than ranking position. Noble reminds us that ranking results isn't just a complex math problem for objectively determining which item should be listed before all the others. Rather, "'ranking' means something very specific in our cultural context in the United States."[9] That is, simply by using the technique of "ranking," search engine designers have told American users to approach results in a particular way. And as Google's dominance continues throughout the world, we are exporting this way of interacting with ranked results.

Search Engines, Objectivity, and Trust

Search engines and the algorithms behind them have become so much a part of everyday life that we often don't take into account how they work or whether they might be wrong. Rather, search tools are inherently trusted, especially general purpose search engines like Google, despite being multinational corporations that have effectively privatized information retrieval.[10] The reasons for this trust vary, but it's one that the search engine companies actively cultivate. While still at Google, Marissa Mayer hinted at the relationship between the simple interface and the necessary trust that users could have in Google. She described the search engine as,

> very, very complicated technology, but behind a very simple interface. Our users don't need to understand how complicated the technology and the development work that happens behind us is. What they do need to understand is that they can just go to a box, type what they want, and get answers.[11]

While she wanted us to know that Google handles the complexity, she emphasizes that the simplicity of the user interface breeds trust in the users.

---

9   Safiya Umoja Noble and Sarah T. Roberts, "Engine Failure: Safiya Umoja Noble and Sarah T. Roberts on the Problems of Platform Capitalism," *Logic* 3 (2017): 91.

10   Noble, *Algorithms of Oppression,* 51.

11   Siva Vaidhyanathan, *The Googlization of Everything (And Why We Should Worry)* (Berkeley: University of California Press, 2011), 54.

Notice that she doesn't say that searching in Google gives you "results" or "possibilities." Instead, she says Google provides "answers."

This is a common refrain from Google, which is the only search provider to have also emphasized that its results are "algorithmically-generated," "objective," and "never manipulated."[12] In 2016 Google's help pages claimed that search algorithms were "computer programs that look for clues to give you back exactly what you want."[13]

This image of neutral objectivity, coupled with Google's market dominance, makes it incredibly powerful. The journalist Noah Berlatsky argues that Google "arguably has more power over knowledge and information than television or radio in the modern era."[14] Note that he is not comparing the *Internet,* a communication medium, to another communication medium like television and radio. He is comparing a multinational corporation to a communication medium.

As early as 2005, the Pew Internet and American Life Project noted that the public was beginning to see search engines as a form of public institution like the legal, journalistic, and educational institutions we are "unusually reliant on."[15] This perception has only increased over the past decade and a half. In 2012, Pew researchers noted that users trusted search engines to provide information, and were generally satisfied with the performance of search tools.[16] Almost three-quarters of search engine users in the United States said "most or all of the information they find as they use

---

12   Benjamin Edelman and Benjamin Lockwood, "Measuring Bias in 'Organic' Web Search," January 9, 2011, http://www.benedelman.org/searchbias/.

13   Tufekci, "The Real Bias Built in at Facebook."

14   Noah Berlatsky, "Google Search Algorithms Are Not Impartial. They Can Be Biased, Just Like Their Designers," *NBC News: Think,* February 21, 2018, https://www.nbcnews.com/think/opinion/google-search-algorithms-are-not-impartial-they-are-biased-just-ncna849886.

15   Deborah Fallows, "Search Engine Users: Internet Searchers Are Confident, Satisfied and Trusting—but They Are Also Unaware and Naïve," *Pew Internet and American Life Project,* January 23, 2005, http://pewinternet.org/Reports/2005/Search-Engine-Users/8-Conclusions/Conclusions.aspx.

16   Kristen Purcell, Joanna Brenner, and Lee Rainie, "Search Engine Use 2012," *Pew Internet and American Life Project,* March 9, 2012, http://www.pewinternet.org/2012/03/09/search-engine-use-2012/.

search engines is accurate and trustworthy."[17] And two-thirds believed that "search engines are a fair and unbiased source of information."[18] Google has actively cultivated this trust through its marketing and messaging, but it also uses other techniques to convince users to trust its results.

Google's simple interface works to enhance the users' trust in the search engine. (And this interface—a single search box on a sparse background—has been copied by nearly every other search engine, as well as by all library discovery systems and most library research databases.) According to Miriam Sweeney, "the simple, sparse design [of Google] works to obscure the complexity of the interface, making the result appear purely scientific and data-driven."[19] Noble emphasizes how that simple design "conveys, through its aesthetic, the idea that there's nothing going on."[20] Journalist Stephen Levy wrote about how Marissa Mayer emphasized the importance of designing the tools to look like humans were not involved. She reportedly told a group of designers, "'It looks like a human was involved in choosing what went where. ... Google products are machine-driven. They're created by machines. And that is what makes us powerful.'"[21] The irony is that she was saying this to a group of humans who were, in fact, designing the interface.

This simple design also works to shape our interactions with the search engine, in ways that may make the results seem more relevant to our searches. Noble notes that the simplified design forces users to simplify the way they think about the concept they are searching for in order to fit the design of the system.[22] That is, what we type does not reflect the totality

---

17   Purcell, Brenner, and Rainie.

18   Purcell, Brenner, and Rainie.

19   Miriam Sweeney, "Not just a pretty (inter)face: A critical analysis of Microsoft's 'Ms. Dewey'" (PhD diss., University of Illinois at Urbana-Champaign, 2013), 78.

20   Noble and Roberts, "Engine Failure," 94.

21   Lohr, *Data-ism,* 206–07.

22   Safiya Umoja Noble, "Google Search: Hyper-Visibility as a Means of Rendering Black Women and Girls Invisible," *InVisible Culture: An Electronic Journal for Visual Culture* 19 (October 29, 2013): https://ivc.lib.rochester.edu/google-search-hyper-visibility-as-a-means-of-rendering-black-women-and-girls-invisible/; See also Noble, *Algorithms of Oppression,* 37–38.

of how we think. But the simple design aesthetic of search engines extends beyond the search box onto the results screen. As early as 2008, S. Shyam Sundar worried about how interface design would affect a users' ability to assess the credibility of results.[23] In the same year, a study by the researchers Soo Young Rieh and Brian Hilligoss from the University of Michigan School of Information shows the degree of trust in Google was often due to its design features. One student explained "Google appears to be more credible because it does not have any of the other stuff."[24] The other stuff, presumably, were other design elements that make an interface seem more cluttered or complex. The simplified design makes search results seem almost natural (which, ironically, are seen as the result of algorithmic work and not "human manipulation"). The term for these kinds of search results is "organic search," which uses the metaphor of natural, pure, unmanipulated food to give an extra patina of trustworthiness to Google's search results. Researchers Anna Jobin and Malte Ziewitz, challenging the "organic" metaphor, emphasize that "any search results page is a carefully constructed product of design and use. There is nothing inherently 'organic' about a list of computationally generated links."[25]

But there is still more than just marketing and the simple interface to our trust of Google. The company actively reminds us that its tools are making choices and selections through algorithms, rather than through human curation or judgment. The footer of Google News, for instance, until recently reminded us that the news articles were "selected by an algorithm," a direct challenge to other major news sources who rely on human curation to choose the content on their home pages.

The idea is that the computer is an objective observer of the news, rather than a biased editorializer. But as the legal scholar Danielle Citron

---

23   S. Shyam Sundar, "The MAIN Model: A Heuristic Approach to Understanding Technology Effects on Credibility," in *Digital media, youth, and credibility*, eds. Miriam J. Metzger and Andrew J. Flanagin (Cambridge, MA: MIT Press, 2008), 76.

24   Soo Young Rieh and Brian Hilligoss, "College Students Credibility Judgments in the Information-Seeking Process," in *Digital Media, Youth, and credibility*, eds. Miriam J. Metzger and Andrew J. Flanagin (Cambridge, MA: MIT Press, 2008), 61.

25   Anna Jobin and Malte Ziewitz, "Organic Search: How Metaphors Help Cultivate the Web," Alexander Von Humbolt Institut Für Internet und Gesellschaft, March 6, 2018, https://www.hiig.de/en/organic-search-metaphors-help-cultivate-web/.

reminds us, "we trust algorithms because we think of them as objective, whereas the reality is that humans craft those algorithms and can embed in them all sorts of biases and perspectives."[26] The Google News algorithm itself was written by people who had to made choices about what attributes of a news story are important enough to consider for inclusion on the Google News homepage. That itself is an editorializing decision, but because the human selection process is hidden behind a layer of computer code, it isn't visible to the public. In addition, the news stories Google News is selecting from were written by humans and were chosen to appear on their respective news outlets' websites by human editors.

Gillespie reminds us that search engines have many often competing priorities behind the processes that determine what results are retrieved and how they are ranked. They must "satisfy not just the user, but the aims of the provider, their understanding of relevance or newsworthiness or public import, and the particular demands of their business model."[27] That Google is one of the highest valued companies in history is no accident—it serves up advertisements throughout its interface every time a search is run to the tune of nearly 4 billion a day.[28] This has led many to argue that Google is actually an advertising company, rather than an information company.[29] Google claims to be neither, instead insisting it is a "technology company," a meaningless category that allows it and other companies to avoid regulations that apply to existing business sectors.

One real issue at play here is where to point the finger when incorrect or biased information is returned by Google. In early 2018, *The Guardian* reported that Google searches for abortion providers were suggesting "Pregnancy Crisis Centers," which are in fact non-medical, anti-abortion

---

26   Luke Dormehl, *The Formula: How Algorithms Solve All Our Problems—and Create More* (New York: Penguin, 2014), 150.

27   Gillespie, "Can an Algorithm Be Wrong?"

28   Internet Live Stats, "Internet Live Stats."

29   Zenyp Tufekci, "YouTube, the Great Radicalizer," *New York Times,* March 10, 2018, https://www.nytimes.com/2018/03/10/opinion/sunday/youtube-politics-radical.html; O'Neil, *Weapons of Math Destruction,* 184; Noble, *Algorithms of Oppression,* 28.

organizations that actively discourage abortions.[30] Four years earlier, Google had removed the ads for 'Pregnancy Crisis Centers' that were shown on searches related to abortion by accusing the centers of falsely claiming they offered medical services. Molly Duane, a staff attorney with the Center for Reproductive Rights, lamented "the internet should be a place where you can get full information, not where women are deliberately deceived about their options."[31] Here Duane betrayed her faith in Google's role as a trustworthy gatekeeper by conflating it with the entire internet. In another case, the journalist Rachel Abrams wrote of the time-consuming challenge of trying to get Google to update its Knowledge Graph panel about Rachel Abrams, which claimed that she was dead (she was not).[32] The problem seemed to be a conflation of two different writers with a fairly common name: Rachel Abrams. Her incorrect information was fixed only after she noted that she was writing an article for the *New York Times* about the experience. Google never offered an explanation for the issue, but did offer her a lot of advice for tricking their automated systems into correcting the information. Even Google seems to trust its own algorithms more than the possibility of human intervention.

Despite all this, it is clear that the public sees algorithmic objectivity as a real phenomenon. In 2017, the communications marketing firm Edelman ran a survey that found that 59 percent of respondents trusted the news they received from search engines, while only 41 percent trusted a human editor.[33] This is despite the fact that those news stories that show up in your web search are themselves hosted on the websites of the mainstream media outlets. What this suggests is that people are more likely to trust a news article if they find them in Google than if they find the *exact*

---

30   Sam Levin, "Google Search Results for Abortion Services Promote Anti-Abortion Centers," *The Guardian,* February 13, 2018, https://www.theguardian.com/world/2018/feb/13/abortions-near-me-google-search-results-anti-pro-life-groups-promote.

31   Levin.

32   Rachel Abrams, "Google Thinks I'm Dead. (I Know Otherwise.)," *New York Times,* December 16, 2017, https://www.nytimes.com/2017/12/16/business/google-thinks-im-dead.html.

33   "2017 Edelman Trust Barometer—Global Results," Slideshare.net, January 15, 2017, https://www.slideshare.net/EdelmanInsights/2017-edelman-trust-barometer-global-results-71035413.

same article on the news outlet's website. The implication is that by appearing in Google results, Google has somehow vetted the article to be more trustworthy, as if Google's search algorithms themselves are becoming the arbiters of truth.

Certainly some of this pixie dust that Google adds to content to make it more trustworthy comes from the persistent marketing for search engines (and Google's products in particular) as objective tools that remove the pesky inefficiencies and biases that humans introduce into the information-seeking process. Before the adoption of search engines, to find information on a topic you might turn to a set of print encyclopedias with articles written by experts, or consult your local librarian, who would direct you to relevant sources.

But Google has upended this, making it as easy as reaching in your pocket to answer questions from the quotidian to the complex. Library Science literature is littered with feverish attempts to convince public library patrons, undergraduates, grad students, and faculty members alike to come to the library to do research rather than starting with Google. In the past decade, the nearly ubiquitous adoption of discovery services (which are often compared favorably to Google by their creators) has been a new approach for libraries. Rather than insisting on the expertise of the profession and recommending the discipline-specific resources that have been created and refined by experts over decades, we instead created a virtual honeypot, our own Google-like interface to make our users feel at home in the academic search environment.

The faith in the inherent objectivity of search algorithms (and social media algorithms) was evident in the run up to the Fall 2018 midterm elections in the United States. Wary of their forecasted poor showing in the election, and facing the possibility of losing control of the House, President Donald Trump and the Republican Party accused Google of deliberately biasing its search algorithms against conservative voices.[34] Much of this played out against the backdrop of many technology companies banning the right-wing ideologue Alex Jones and his Infowars.com website from their platforms, including Google, Facebook, Apple, and, reluctantly weeks later, Twitter. In 2014 a similar situation happened at Facebook when former employees accused the humans that chose the "Trending Topics" for

---

34 Wakabayashi and Kang, "It's Google's Turn in Washington's Glare."

the site of suppressing conservative voices. Notice that no one accused the algorithms themselves of being biased; rather, they accused the companies of deliberately biasing the algorithms against conservative viewpoints, or of humans interfering in the workings of the algorithms. In both cases, writes journalist Jack Nicas in the *New York Times,* "the companies have tried to deflect that criticism by letting algorithms take control."[35] The implication, of course, is that left to their own devices algorithms would not be biased against right or left. They would be neutral.

Ranking and Objectivity

Scholars have shown that this inherent trust isn't reserved simply for Google in particular—it is built into the very way that search works, and in particular, the idea of ranking. Google's search results list, which "ranks" pages from the most "relevant" on down, has become the norm for search engines. Bing, Yahoo!, DuckDuckGo, as well as library search tools like Primo, Summon, WorldCat Discovery, EDS, and nearly every OPAC on the market now rank search results in a hierarchical list based on "relevance." This isn't to claim that Google invented the hierarchical ranking of search results—it merely normalized it.[36]

We saw that search engines are implicitly trusted, and this trust is despite the fact that none of them will tell you why it chose any of your

---

35 Jack Nicas, "Apple's Radical Approach to News: Humans Over Machines," *New York Times,* October 25, 2018, https://www.nytimes.com/2018/10/25/technology/apple-news-humans-algorithms.html.

36 Search results haven't always been ranked by "relevance" (something we will examine in more detail in Chapter 3). As recently as 2008, some library OPACs listed results in system or acquisitions order. Singapore Librarian and blogger Aaron Tay noted that "I remember explaining to a colleague in 2007 that traditionally Boolean searches did not rank results by relevancy as in theory all results can be considered equally relevant as they meet the search criteria but she didn't believe me." Aaron Tay, "How Is Google Different From Traditional Library OPACs & Databases?," May 8, 2012, http://musingsaboutlibrarianship.blogspot.com/2012/05/how-is-google-different-from.html. Even today, most search engines use some variant of "relevant" as the default ranking. Hipmunk.com, the travel site, ranks its flight results by "Agony," least to greatest. "Agony" here is merely a way of encoding assumptions about the relevancy of results—that flights with the shortest total time and the fewest layovers are more relevant to users.

results or why they are precisely ordered in the way they are. In the words of Pasquale, these algorithms are "black boxes," proprietary assets of intellectual property that the search companies protect as a trade secret.[37] We do know some things about how certain search algorithms work. For instance, we know that PageRank, the original "innovation" of Google's search algorithm, looks at how many other sites link to your site in order to assign it a ranking, based on the practice in information science of citation analysis.[38] And scholars have worked on "reverse engineering" why search algorithms display certain results, which will be a major factor in this study of library discovery tools.[39]

According to psychology researchers Robert Epstein and Ronald Robertson, "people trust search engine companies to assign higher ranks to the results best suited to their needs, even though users generally have no idea how results get ranked."[40] And this trust is granted regardless of the content. Over a decade ago, a group of researchers from Cornell and Google led by Thorsten Joachims showed that users had a "trust bias" for highly ranked items, "even if those abstracts are less relevant than other abstracts

---

37 Pasquale, *The Black Box Society*. Pasquale did not invent this term, which has a long history in Science and Technology Studies (STS). The term is mostly associated with the work of the philosopher Bruno Latour, who wrote about the "black boxing" of scientific ideas, where they were made to seem like stand-alone truths and the human work of uncovering them was hidden from view. See Bruno Latour and Steve Woolgar, *Laboratory Life: The Construction of Scientific Facts* (Princeton, NJ: Princeton University Press, 1986).

38 Sergey Brin and Larry Page, "The Anatomy of a Large-Scale Hypertextual Web Search Engine," *Computer Networks and ISDN Systems* 30, no. 1 (1998), http://infolab.stanford.edu/~backrub/google.html. PageRank has evolved quite a bit over the past twenty years, and is only one of several hundred factors Google takes into account when ranking results.

39 For Twitter's Trending Topics algorithm, see Gillespie, "Can an Algorithm Be Wrong?"; for Google's Search algorithms, see Noble, "Google Search: Hyper-Visibility as a Means of Rendering Black Women and Girls Invisible" and Noble, *Algorithms of Oppression*; For Facebook's EdgeRank algorithm, see Tania Bucher, "Want to Be on the Top? Algorithmic Power and the Threat of Invisibility on Facebook," *New Media & Society* 14, no. 7 (2012): 1164–180, https://doi.org/10.1177%2F1461444812440159.

40 Robert Epstein and Ronald Robertson, "The Search Engine Manipulation Effect (SEME) and Its Possible Impact on the Outcomes of Elections," *Proceedings of the National Academy of Sciences of the United States* 112, no. 33 (2015): E4512.

the user viewed."[41] For more than half of the searches in the study, users didn't even *look* at the fourth result or greater. That is, rather than assessing the relevance of individual results on their own merits, the very placement of a result in the hierarchical ranking appears to be one of the most important factors in whether a user will click on it. (This is not news to the Search Engine Optimization (SEO) businesses.) Since users rarely go beyond the first page of searches, if a site is ranked high enough to be seen by users, Halavais notes that "the mere fact that a search engine suggested it lends it credibility."[42] And Noble notes that "the legitimacy of websites' ranking and credibility [in Google] is simply taken for granted."[43]

Noble writes in *Algorithms of Oppression* about Dylann Roof, the white supremacist who murdered nine African Americans in a Charleston, South Carolina church in June of 2015. Roof wrote a manifesto that he published online, noting that he used Google to search for information on "black on white crime," after reading the phrase on a Wikipedia page about Trayvon Martin, an unarmed black teenager that was shot and killed by a security guard in Florida. Roof was shown highly ranked results from the white supremacist website of the Council of Conservative Citizens.[44] But why would Google rank a hate site higher than a less-biased source of information? According to Carole Cadwalladr, a journalist writing for *The Guardian,* it is because Google "reward[s] popular results over authoritative ones."[45]

Cadwalladr started to type a search into Google, beginning "did the hol" and was presented with Google's top autosuggest result, "Did the Holocaust happen?" (Autosuggest is an algorithm that pulls common searches

41   Thorsten Joachims et al., "Evaluating the Accuracy of Implicit Feedback From Clicks and Query Reformulations in Web Search," *ACM Transactions on Information Systems* 25, no. 2 (2007): 3.

42   Halavais, *Search Engine Society,* 42.

43   Noble, *Algorithms of Oppression,* 155.

44   David A. Graham, "The White-Supremicist Group That Inspired a Racist Manifesto," *The Atlantic,* June 22, 2015, https://www.theatlantic.com/politics/archive/2015/06/council-of-conservative-citizens-dylann-roof/396467/.

45   Carole Cadwalladr, "How to Bump Holocaust Deniers Off Google's Top Spot? Pay Google," *The Guardian,* December 17, 2016, https://www.theguardian.com/technology/2016/dec/17/holocaust-deniers-google-search-top-spot.

from around the world as you type.) The top result for this suggested search was a link to the neo-Nazi white-supremacist website Stormfront entitled, "Top 10 reasons why the Holocaust didn't happen." When Cadwalladr contacted Google about the issue, a Google spokesperson responded in a way that shows how much faith Google has in its algorithms: "Search is a reflection of the content that exists on the web. The fact that hate sites appear in search results in no way means that Google endorses these views."[46]

Here Google is imagining that they do not shape how its users understand the world through its awesome power in deciding what to show and what not to show. This is especially problematic when we consider the "trust bias" of how users interact with search. Indeed, Noble emphasizes that "the public believes that what rises to the top in search is either the most popular or the most credible or both."[47]

In March of 2018, librarian Lisa Rabey tweeted about a search she found problematic on Google:

> Bias in Google: Do a search for "famous women in history" and get 95% white ladies like Amelia Erhart and Elizabeth I. Add in "black" to that search string and get Oprah, Michelle Obama, and Beyonce because apparently black women didn't make history until the 20th century.[48]

This happens because Google inserts a Knowledge Graph card at the top of the page with images of women who meet the search criteria. Why was there only one black woman in the results for "famous women in history," Rosa Parks? In the lone reply from Rabey's nearly 3,000 followers, Eileen Clancy summed up this new kind of algorithmic reality: "Don't want to fave that, but have to for visibility purposes, because algorithms."[49]

---

46   Cadwalladr.

47   Noble, *Algorithms of Oppression,* 32.

48   Lisa Rabey, Twitter Post, March 11, 2018, 5:00pm,
     https://twitter.com/heroineinabook/status/972985545314971648.

49   Eileen Clancy, Twitter Post, March 11, 2018, 5:56pm,
     https://mobile.twitter.com/clancynewyork/status/972999819697455104.

These results, which are just a sample of the problems that I read about on a daily basis, are troubling in themselves. But they are also problematic in that they reinforce structural biases in our society—racism, sexism, and antisemitism—whitewashed by the machinery that is supposed to show us objective truth. Silicon Valley is a notoriously sexist place, employing mostly white men to write the algorithms that frame these objective judgments.[50] Pasquale emphasizes that despite these claims of objectivity, search engines "are constantly making value-laden, controversial decisions. They help create the world they claim to merely 'show' us."[51] Halavais warns of the authoritarian nature of "ranking implementations that directly measure and reinforce authority,"[52] noting that they will reinforce existing power structures. As I discussed earlier, Noble reminds us that ranking itself is not a neutral and objective thing: it has different cultural meanings in different places. What is more, she emphasizes that "search results are not tied to a multiplicity of perspectives."[53] What does it say about an industry dominated by white men that creates tools to deliver "answers" that reinforce centuries-old racist, sexist, and anti-semitic stereotypes? (Chapter 4 is dedicated to diving deeply into this question of bias.)

As of October 2018, a search for "Did the holocaust happen?" returns a Knowledge Graph box about the Holocaust, with 10 factual sites about the Holocaust or Holocaust denial. While no longer on the first page of results, the Stormfront page is still online. Why have the search results changed? As of October 2018, a search for "famous women in history" still shows mostly white women, and if you add the qualifier "black," you no longer get a Knowledge Graph tile at all, implying that the search is no longer important. Rabey does not write for a major media outlet. Does change happen at Google only when there is a high-profile media story critical of its algorithm-centered defense of its search results? We'll probably never know, suggests Noble. All we can do is remember that "human beings are

50   See, for instance, Katherine Losse, *The Boy Kings: A Journey to the Heart of the Social Network* (New York: Free Press, 2014).

51   Pasquale, *The Black Box Society,* 61.

52   Halavais, *Search Engine Society,* 104.

53   Noble, *Algorithms of Oppression,* 118.

designing them [algorithms] and that they are not up for public discussion, except as we engage in critique and protest."[54]

Advertising

Any discussion of Google's (or any search engine's) claim to be a neutral and objective platform would not be complete without touching on their reason to exist: advertising. Almost all search engines use tracking scripts to better understand which links users click and how users respond to design changes.[55] But these scripts also allow search engines to connect our search behavior to other behavior around the web. Google provides a free analytics program that websites can install in order to better understand how their users interact with their sites. But Google also gets to follow users around the web. All this data (what Tim Cook, CEO of Apple, called the "data industrial complex"[56]) is then used to precisely target advertisements to users based on what they have searched for, looked at on other sites, or from inferences based on the data of others. And since Google also owns many other popular services, like Gmail, YouTube, Google Drive, and even the most popular computer in the K-12 market, the Chromebook,[57] they collect data from these services and as you move around the web.

Increasingly, Google has also begun to incorporate this trove of data into the search results for its users. Tailoring search results to fit the personal data Google has collected about you is a boon to users, the company says. But researchers Martin Feuz, Matthew Fuller, and Felix Stalder found that personalization was also a boon to advertisers.[58] What's more, the impact

---

54   Noble, 4.

55   Halavais, *Search Engine Society,* 47.

56   Jack Nicas, "The Week in Tech: Apple Goes on the Attack," *New York Times,* October 26, 2018, https://www.nytimes.com/2018/10/26/technology/apple-time-cook-europe.html.

57   Zenyp Tufekci, Twitter Post, March 12, 2018, 9:52am, https://twitter.com/zeynep/status/973240286120878085.

58   Martin Feuz, Matthew Fuller, and Felix Stalder, "Personal Web Searching in the Age of Semantic Capitalism: Diagnosing the Mechanisms of Personalization," *First Monday* 16, no. 2 (2011), http://firstmonday.org/ojs/index.php/fm/article/view/3344/2766.

of the kinds of results that Google shows to people are predicated on Google's own sorting mechanism. In their words, "Google is actively matching people to groups."[59] This results in limiting the possibilities that are presented to users, "more or less subtly pushing users to see the world according to criteria predefined by Google."[60] Google's role as an advertising company shapes the kinds of information that it presents to its users. As Noble contends, Google is "an advertising platform [and is] not intended as a public information resource."[61] O'Neil concurs, and notes that despite its real purpose of "raising revenue," search results "could have a dramatic effect on what people learn and how they vote."[62]

Google Search's design choices here also help to burnish the companies reputation for objectivity. By labeling sponsors' advertisements as such, they give the impression that the rest of the results, the so-called "organic" search results, are free from manipulation. Jobin and Ziewitz note that this allows the company to "claim that they are not accepting money in exchange for influence while also generating revenue through ads displayed in those coveted first spots."[63] Cadwalladr's research also highlights Google's tendencies to rank results by popularity, as I noted above. This is because "organizing searches by popularity is appealing to Google's advertisers."[64]

This issue extends to all of Google's properties, not just search. As I discussed in Chapter 1, YouTube has been under fire for the past year for using its autoplay feature to promote videos that get more "engagement" in the form of time watched, likes, and comments than others. It just so happens that videos that meet this criteria are often radicalization videos, conspiracy theories, hate speech, and more. No one at Google has sat down and tried to deliberately program offensive or radicalized search results. But by training the algorithms to focus on values like engagement in order to generate more advertising revenue, they came to the same result. As Tufekci

---

59 Fuez, Fuller, and Stadler.

60 Fuez, Fuller, and Stadler.

61 Noble, *Algorithms of Oppression*, 28.

62 O'Neil, *Weapons of Math Destruction*, 184.

63 Jobin and Ziewitz, "Organic Search."

64 Berlatsky, "Google Search Algorithms Are Not Impartial."

notes, "for all its lofty rhetoric, Google is an advertising broker, selling our attention to companies that will pay for it. The longer people stay on You-Tube, the more money Google makes."[65]

This is an important point, that Google is first and foremost a business. It isn't an actual public utility, although it is often thought of and referred to as such. Google's only responsibility is to its shareholders. It does not actually need to put the public good before maximizing profits. In the runup to the 2018 midterm elections in the United States, conservatives assumed that the role of Google is to be the objective arbiter of truth in the world. Google has encouraged this thinking, claiming that their algorithms are objective in nearly all its communications, even internally. Marissa Mayer, speaking on behalf of Google's engineers, explained Google's mission as "we're trying to build a virtual mirror of the world at all times."[66]

Search engines play a huge role in how we learn. They have power to show us some results and hide others. As Michael Sacasas, the director of the Center for the Study of Ethics and Technology notes, "the technology directs and guides our perception and our attention. It says to us 'Look at this here not that over there' or 'Look at this thing in this way.'"[67] This guidance hides behind a veil of neutrality but has real effects in the world outside of our computer screens. Pasquale agrees, arguing that this power allows search engines to "mediate how we perceive."[68] Yet users rarely notice this power. For most of us, search engines seem like an objective way to "answer our most profound and trivial questions."[69] But this belief in search engines' objectivity is just that: a belief. According to Halavais, search engines "have become an object of faith."[70]

---

65   Tufekci, "YouTube, the Great Radicalizer."

66   M. G. Siegler, "Marissa Mayer's Next Big Thing: 'Contextual Discovery'—Google Results Without Search," *TechCrunch,* December 8, 2010, http://techcrunch.com/2010/12/08/googles-next-big-thing.

67   Michael Sacasas, "The Ethics of Technological Mediation," November 18, 2017, https://thefrailestthing.com/2017/11/18/the-ethics-of-technological-mediation/.

68   Pasquale, *The Black Box Society,* 58.

69   Halavais, *Search Engine Society,* 2.

70   Halavais, 2.

Noble also explores how search engines help to shape the way we perceive the world. She notes that a list of search results has "symbolic and material meaning,"[71] rather than just being a neutral list of links. That faith that we put in search engines has elevated the list into something that has meaning apart from the content of each result. She examines how this perceived meaning of search results has become nearly ubiquitous without anyone noticing. "Algorithms," she writes, "function as an artifact of culture."[72]

Her work understanding how Google portrays women of color through search results (mostly, she learned, as pornographic objects[73]) also helps to highlight the cultural meaning-making that happens when search results are interpreted. Whereas search presents results in a seemingly neutral format, showing content as just websites or links,

> the language and terminologies used to describe results on the Internet in commercial search engines often obscure the fact that commodified forms of representation are being transacted on the web and that these commercial transactions are not random or without meaning as simply websites.[74]

That is, Google results show you one particular viewpoint while pretending to not have a viewpoint at all. We must understand search results as contextual rather than as groups of isolated words. Noble reminds us that search results "can be legitimated only in social, political, and historical context."[75]

As I write this, the news is full of reports of hate crimes committed by two men who are said to have been "radicalized online." Cesar Sayoc mailed over a dozen bombs to prominent Democrats throughout the United States, supposedly because of the rhetoric of President Donald Trump,

---

71 Noble, *Algorithms of Oppression,* 84.

72 Noble, 85.

73 Safiya Umoja Noble, "Missed Connections: What Search Engines Say About Women," *Bitch* 1, no. 54 (2012): 36–41; Noble, "Google Search"; Noble, *Algorithms of Oppression.*

74 Noble, *Algorithms of Oppression,* 106.

75 Noble, 45.

who repeatedly calls political opponents "dangerous" and "evil."[76] A few days after he was arrested, Robert D. Bowers walked into a synagogue in Pittsburgh and murdered 11 people, supposedly because of conspiracy theories he read online claiming that Jewish people perpetrated September 11th.[77] We have already looked at Dylann Roof, who murdered nine in Charleston, South Carolina. Dozens of Al-Qaeda and ISIS sympathizers have been accused of being "radicalized online" over the past fifteen years. These are just the latest examples of users looking for information online in supposedly neutral environments, and coming away with radicalized beliefs that spill out and have real-world effects.

Google has repeatedly deferred to its algorithms to explain objectionable or false content showing up prominently in search results.[78] Rich Matta, the chief executive of the website Reputation Defender, notes that it is very difficult for the average user to distinguish what is true and what is false on a search results page. "Search results these days are your first impression," he says.[79] This is especially important as more and more people gravitate towards search technologies for information, which have, Noble points out, "political, social [and] economic consequences."[80] As search technologies operate within culture and history as part of a system, we shouldn't be surprised that changing one aspect of the system will have effects on other parts.[81] Noble writes that search results "structure knowledge," and that

---

76   Philip Rucker, "Amid Incendiary Rhetoric, Targets of Trump's Words Become Targets of Bombs," *The Washington Post,* October 24, 2018, https://www.washingtonpost.com/politics/amid-incendiary-rhetoric-targets-of-trumps-words-become-targets-of-bombs/2018/10/24/9dddc97c-d7c7-11e8-83a2-d1c3da28d6b6_story.html.

77   Campbell Robertson, Christopher Mele, and Sabrina Taverinse, "11 Killed in Synagogue Massacre; Suspect Charged With 29 Counts," *The New York Times,* October 27, 2018, https://www.nytimes.com/2018/10/27/us/active-shooter-pittsburgh-synagogue-shooting.html.

78   See Cadwalladr, "How to Bump Holocaust Deniers Off Google's Top Spot?"; Noble, "Google Search."

79   Abrams, "Google Thinks I'm Dead."

80   Noble, *Algorithms of Oppression,* 9.

81   Alex Soojung-Kim Pang, *The Distraction Addiction* (New York: Little Brown, 2013), 157.

search results "create their own material reality,"[82] as we have seen with the extreme examples of Dylann Roof, Cesar Sayoc, and Robert D. Bowers. And more than just offering a patina of mathematical objectivity, she argues that ranking "is itself information that also reflects the political, social, and cultural values of the society that search engine companies operate in."[83] So without even considering the information presented in the content of the first three results, merely the fact that a hierarchical list is presented tells a user that the first three results are likely the most popular or credible.

And since Google's algorithm takes into account how popular a site is, the assumptions behind that site will then be glossed over with credibility, as in Cadwalladr's search for "was the holocaust real?" When Cadwalladr started a search with "are jews," Google suggested "Are Jews evil?", which, she noted, was "not a question I'd ever thought of asking."[84] It is not only through its "organic" search results that Google shapes our perception of the world. As Internet Ethics program director at the Markkula Center for Applied Ethics Irina Raicu notes, "via autocomplete [also called autosuggest], Google is a provider of questions, as well as answers. And Google makes decisions about both."[85] In February of 2018, within a day of the shootings at Parkland High School in Florida, autosuggest was implying that "Parkland students [are] actors" and that one of the students, David Hogg, was a "crisis actor."[86] By suggesting these results for popular searches, Google's autosuggest algorithm acts to shape what kinds of questions it is possible to ask.

Different aspects of Google's toolkit shape the world you see in different ways. The author Alex Soojung-Kim Pang has written about the Victorian art critic Philip Hamerton, who "argued that watercolors teach you to

---

82   Noble, *Algorithms of Oppression*, 148.

83   Noble, 148.

84   Carole Cadwalladr, "Google, Democracy and the Truth About Internet Search," *The Guardian,* December 4, 2016, https://www.theguardian.com/technology/2016/dec/04/google-democracy-truth-internet-search-facebook.

85   Irina Raicu, "Autocompleted," *Markkula Center for Applied Ethics,* May 9, 2017, https://www.scu.edu/ethics/internet-ethics-blog/autocompleted/.

86   Jonathan Albright, "#NotOKGoogle Search Suggestions: 2018 Edition," *Medium* (blog), February 21, 2018, https://medium.com/@d1gi/notokgoogle-search-suggestions-2018-edition-ba09eaf49fc2.

see the world in terms of spaces and tones, while the pencil encourages you to see it in terms of hard lines and shadows…Any technology—even eyeglasses—has its biases."[87] In search engines, autosuggest encourages us to think of our questions in the same terms that others have used, while results encourage us to think in terms of "better" or "worse" answers.

The search engines' power to shape the world does not only extend to the users who are looking for information. By returning "objective" results about the world, they determine identity for people who may already be marginalized. In Noble's research on searches for "black girls" that returned primarily porn websites, black girls' "identity is subject to control by people looking for porn."[88] Lilian Black, the chair of The Holocaust Survivors Friendship Association told Cadwalladr that search engines "shape people's thinking and are disparaging the memory of people like my grandparents who were gassed."[89] The trouble with trying to understand people and culture through search engines, writes Noble, is that search engines

> oversimplify complex phenomena. They obscure any struggle over understanding, and they can mask history. Search results can reframe our thinking and deny us the ability to engage deeply with essential information and knowledge we need, knowledge that has traditionally been learned through teachers, books, history, and experience.[90]

This extends to all forms of search, as Noble shows searches for "black girls" and "asian girls" consistently return hypersexualized content and Cadwalladr shows how antisemitism can surface in popularity-based autosuggest algorithms. In later chapters, I will explore how these same kinds of identity issues are at the heart of biased results in library discovery systems, like the result shown in Figure 2.2, where a known item search for a book on the information needs of LGBTQ youth in Summon returns only two results: the book, and a text on "mental illness."

---

87   Pang, *The Distraction Addiction,* 146.

88   Noble, "Google Search."

89   Cadwalladr, "How to Bump Holocaust Deniers Off Google's Top Spot?"

90   Noble, *Algorithms of Oppression,* 116.

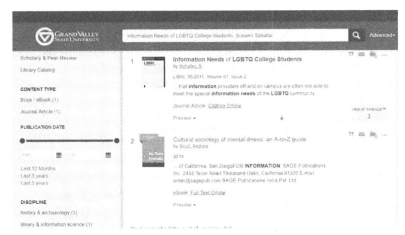

Figure 2.2   Search results linking mental illness and LGBTQ youth in Summon. Screenshot by Gayle Schaub.

These kinds of correlations in results work to shape the perceptions we have of groups of people, which in return control the types of identities that people can claim for themselves. If Google is showing everyone search results for hypersexualized "black girls," then it's not just a matter of black girls "shrugging off" this stereotype. Google has shaped the perception of what black girls can be not only for black girls, but for all of us. And in library discovery, a place where libraries have long argued that trustworthiness should exceed even that of Google's results, what are the effects of showing results about mental illness when the user searched for information on LGBTQ youth? The technical reasons for these results appearing are less important than the fact that the results here do not include any of the context about the history of biased categorization that LGBTQ people have endured at the hands of the Library of Congress and other arbiters of knowledge management, or the history of bias and oppression from society as a whole. Rather, the result just appears, and as one of only two results, users interpret it as necessarily relevant.

But what ethical responsibilities do the companies that make search engines and search algorithms have to address these problems? Writing a decade ago, Halavais argued that search engine designers "have an ethical obligation to the communities in which they work."[91] But this was long before the age where we realized the extent of fake news, radicalization propaganda, deliberately manipulated information aimed at influencing foreign elections, and systemic racial, gender, and other biases baked into the search process itself. For Halavais, the most pressing question was a response to personalization "who sees what under what circumstances and in what context?"[92] For him, ensuring that everyone had equitable access to the same kinds of reliable information was the most pressing issue. But today, we see many more threats. Personalized search results can do more than just insulate us in our own "filter bubbles," as Eli Pariser dubbed the experience of only ever finding information you agree with.[93] Now, our search results create alternate realities, where onetime fringe theories are treated as verified fact and the anger and violence that results often spills out into our daily lives. The United States Government itself peddles in "alternative facts" that suit the narrative they have chosen. And search engines, with their well-honed patina of objectivity, are a perfect conduit for conveying this information to others.

As we delve into library discovery systems and the different ways in which bias presents itself in the following chapters, we will dig deeper into the kinds of ethical responses that the companies that create search technologies owe the public. But for starters, Google's response to Cadwalladr's antisemitic searches should be unthinkable. Search technologies cannot claim to be both "providing answers" and at the same time just showing the web pages that exist. As Berlatsky asserts, "we need our search engines to help challenge the assumptions of people like [Dylann] Roof, not feed their hate."[94]

It is easy to say that the extent of the issues we've looked at facing general-purpose search engines don't apply to library discovery. But library discovery systems are designed with the explicit intent of facilitating learning, and of helping researchers better understand not only the academic

---

91   Halavais, *Search Engine Society,* 113.

92   Halavais, 118.

93   Eli Pariser, *The Filter Bubble: How the New Personalized Web Is Changing What We Read and How We Think* (New York: Penguin Books, 2012).

94   Berlatsky, "Google Search Algorithms Are Not Impartial."

and professional literature on a given topic, but developing a better understanding of the topic through auxiliary algorithms like Google's Knowledge Graph. But while library discovery systems are different than Google in many ways, there are also striking similarities in the kinds of claims made about the objectivity of these search tools, at times by the vendors that make them, and at times by the libraries that license them.

Chapter 3   Library Discovery

Google, Bing, and other general-purpose search engines are not the only search tools that claim to be neutral and objective. Library search tools also claim these qualities, and often claim to be more trustworthy than their general-purpose counterparts. While general-purpose search tools search a broad selection of content (such as much of the public, open web), library search tools instead focus on a narrow, limited amount of content, usually the items held in a collection or the articles available through licensed subscription databases. Search tools that cast their nets broadly are called "horizontal search," in industry jargon. By contrast, specialty search tools that focus on a limited but deep set of content are called "vertical search."[1]

There are many different kinds of library search tools. Online Public Access Catalogs (OPACs)—like Innovative Interfaces' WebPAC Pro, Sirsi Dynix's Unicorn, or Evergreen's OPAC—allow users to search for books and journals that are owned by the library. Digital collections tools like Omeka or DSpace allow users to search for digitized items in a collection, like photographs, manuscripts, or letters from a special collection. Institutional Repositories like bepress's Digital Commons allow users to search through items that were written or published by authors who are affiliated with the institution. Subscription databases like Lexis Nexis or Academic Search Premier allow users to focus on curated, licensed articles from a wide selection of journals, usually grouped by discipline. Tools like Archives Space allow users to search for finding aids to learn more

---

1   Halavais, *Search Engine Society,* 7.

about non-digitized archival collections. And discovery systems allow users to search through most of the contents of the OPAC, Digital Collections tools, Institutional Repositories, finding aids, and subscription databases from a single search box.

The term "discovery system" does not appear to be well-understood within the library community (or elsewhere, as the Wikipedia page shows, since it only lists the two Ex Libris products, Summon and Primo).[2] Athena Hoeppner, the Discovery Services Librarian at the University of Central Florida, explains that the discovery system is properly called "Web scale discovery," which refers to a "preharvested central index coupled with a richly featured discovery layer providing a single search across a library's local, open access, and subscription collections."[3] The discovery layer is the part of the system that library users interact with, containing the search interface and results screens, while the centralized index contains a wide-variety of content to enable such diverse searching, including "full text and citations from publishers; full text and metadata from open source collections; full text, abstracting, and indexing from aggregators and subscription databases; and MARC from library catalogs."[4] In this study, I will refer to library discovery systems rather than "Web-scale discovery," which I find to be a gimmicky marketing term that muddies the waters of any substantive discussion of these tools. Since the index and the discovery layer are never experienced in isolation, I treat them as a whole.

Library discovery systems are also often referred to as "Google-like" for their centralized indexes that allow users to search across hundreds of different subscription databases from a single search box. (That libraries willingly stopped railing against Google, as they had done for a decade or more, and used it as an aspiration for their own systems shows the power of the public's trust in the search giant.) And there are similarities between library discovery and Google, so the comparison is not undeserved. Both tools use a single search box to suggest that the search process is a simple

---

2   "Discovery System," *Wikipedia*, last modified September 11, 2017, https://en.wikipedia.org/wiki/Discovery_system.

3   Athena Hoeppner, "The Ins and Outs of Evaluating Web-Scale Discovery Services," *Information Today*, April 2012, http://www.infotoday.com/cilmag/apr12/Hoeppner-Web-Scale-Discovery-Services.shtml.

4   Hoeppner.

endeavor. Both give you a single set of results pulled from throughout the entire index, while also allowing you to limit your results to particular formats, such as an image search or limiting only to newspaper articles. And both rely on complex algorithms to determine the relevance of the thousands or millions of items returned for each search. In many cases, library discovery services also have auxilliary algorithms like autosuggest, spelling correction, Knowledge-graph-like reference panels, recommended searches, recommended librarians or research guides. Jane Burke, then a Vice President at ProQuest, spoke in 2010 at the VALA Conference in Australia one year after Summon launched and called library discovery systems "the 'Googlisation' of the library's collections."[5] She also emphasized that the goal of Summon was "aim[ed] squarely at Google as the competitor and to mimic that search engine's characteristics of simple, easy, fast."[6] Not only did library discovery vendors want users to think of discovery as Google-like, the tools were designed to be a direct competitor to Google in the scholarly market.

I lump all library discovery systems together in this comparison, because studies have shown that end users have a hard time distinguishing the user interfaces of the four most prominent discovery systems: Ex Libris' Summon and Primo, OCLC's WorldCat Discovery, and EBSCO's EBSCO Discovery Service (EDS).[7] There are other discovery systems, like the open source VuFind, but my research here is based on the commercial systems with undisclosed search algorithms. VuFind runs on top of another Open Source project, Solr search, and requires a local index[8] rather than a centralized one that can be shared across many different instances. This local index can be populated by a library's catalog records and digital library

---

5   Jane Burke, "Discovery Versus Disintermediation: The New Reality Driven by Today's End-User," Paper presented at the VALA Conference, Melbourne, Australia, February, 2010, http://www.vala.org.au/vala2010/papers2010/VALA2010_57_Burke_Final.pdf.

6   Burke, ""Discovery Versus Disintermediation."

7   Aaron Tay, "Primo and Summon—Same but different?," *Musings About Librarianship* (blog), February 29, 2016, http://musingsaboutlibrarianship.blogspot.com/2016/02/primo-and-summon-same-but-different-i.html.

8   "Indexing," VuFind.org, April 21, 2017, https://vufind.org/wiki/indexing.

items, but will not include commercial article databases like the big four library discovery services do.[9]

There are also some significant differences between Google and library discovery systems, and many of these factor in to our investigation into the effectiveness, accuracy, and fairness of library discovery systems' results. The first and most obvious is that the financial business model of the library discovery system is not based on advertising to users. Noble notes that ad-supported horizontal search tools like Google design "advertising algorithms, not information algorithms."[10] Commercial library discovery providers rely instead on annual subscription rates from individual libraries, each paying tens of thousands of dollars a year to use the discovery system to search their collections. This partially insulates library users from the kinds of invasive surveillance that Google and Bing rely on to profile users in order to serve them with more personalized advertising (and thus generate more revenue). Yet three of the four largest library discovery services are also vendors of aggregated content, and so discovery services may also be a business move to generate more revenue in the subscription market. For years, EBSCO has withheld its complete metadata from being included in Ex Libris' index in Summon and Primo.[11] This is a common issue, as evidenced by a common help entry in Ex Libris's help site: "Why Do I Get an Error Page When Linking Out to EBSCOhost Databases?"[12]

All of the library discovery systems collect usage analytics in order to inform their own design process, as well as showing usage information that is potentially useful to the licensing libraries. And many libraries use third party analytics tools like Google Analytics to track usage, which then

---

9   It is possible to use VuFind with commercial article databases, but it becomes a "wrapper" to the third-party discovery services rather than acting as a discovery service on its own. See "Indexing," VuFind.org.

10   Noble, *Algorithms of Oppression*, 28.

11   Marshall Breeding, "Web-Scale Discovery Services: Finding the Right Balance," *American Libraries*, January 14, 2014, https://americanlibrariesmagazine.org/2014/01/14/web-scale-discovery-services/.

12   "Why Do I Get an Error Page When Linking Out to EBSCOhost Databases?," Ex Libris Knowledge Center, May 18, 2017, https://knowledge.exlibrisgroup.com/Summon/Knowledge_Articles/Why_do_I_get_an_error_page_when_linking_out_to_EBSCOhost_databases.

hands over user data to Google. (This is especially troublesome for universities that also partner with Gmail for their campus mail system. Often these searches are done while logged into Gmail, adding the academic searches to Google's ever-expanding dossier of data about us.) Of course, collecting and then selling data is also a lucrative business in and of itself, and selling data may eventually prove too tempting to the companies that provide discovery systems.

Library discovery is also a much more stable environment than a commercial horizontal search tool. Google and other algorithmically-driven tools are constantly running experiments with their design and algorithms, leading to Seaver's quip, "you can never log into the same Facebook twice."[13] Because library discovery tools are licensed (and often rebranded by) libraries, the commercial providers make changes on a schedule rather than running live experiments. As a Summon customer, GVSU usually has an idea of the changes that Ex Libris will be working on 6 months to a year in advance, and we often have an opportunity to try out new features for a few weeks or months before they go live. What's more, often the new features are able to be turned off at the local level by the licensing library, in case they do not meet the needs of the library or are launched at a time that doesn't fit with the academic calendar or staffing and professional development work.[14] This is helpful in analyzing various discovery services, because you won't have to worry that each search is being run through different search algorithms. Each day you can be fairly certain that you are testing the same algorithm you used yesterday.

This extends to the use of so-called "machine learning" or "artificial intelligence" algorithms to personalize or adapt to user interactions or search terms. I use quotes around these terms because the words "learning" and "intelligence" don't really capture what "machine learning" or "artificial intelligence" mean (they are basically the same thing). Data journalist and Assistant Professor at the Arthur L. Carter Journalism Institute at

---

13   Seaver, "Knowing Algorithms," 6.

14   All of these commercial library discovery services are sold around the world. Academic calendars in the southern hemisphere are quite different than those in the northern hemisphere, making it a challenge to find a time to launch new features that will work for all customers.

NYU Meredith Broussard, in her book *Artificial Unintellgence: How Computers Misunderstand the World*, sums up "machine learning" nicely:

> computer scientists know that machine "learning" is more akin to a metaphor in this case: it means that the machine can improve at its programmed, routine, automated tasks. It doesn't mean that the machine acquires knowledge or wisdom or agency, despite what the term *learning* might imply.[15]

One of the guiding principles of the scientific process (as well as academic research in general) is that others should be able to replicate your work. This extends to finding the sources you used, which is the whole point of a bibliography and citations. If discovery systems used machine learning to change the results based on a user's past interactions with the site, we'd have a hard time teaching new researchers how to find things.[16] This doesn't mean that library discovery vendors won't start implementing machine learning algorithms in the future, but currently most applications of machine learning in search have to do with personalization, which has limited appeal in the academic search market.

One other significant difference between general-purpose search and library discovery is the relationship between the search tool and the content creators. On the open web, website creators use all the tricks and wizardry they can think of to make their content show up as high as possible in a Google search. The entire industry of Search Engine Optimization (SEO) has formed around this important activity, even though it is mostly guesswork. (The writer Merlin Mann once said that SEO was a job where you scream "New Jersey!" at the top of your lungs and then hope that everyone thinks you are Bruce Springsteen for a second.[17]) Google states that one of the main reasons for keeping its algorithms a secret is that they don't want content creators to know how to game the system. In library discovery, the content is written for academic journals, books, trade publications,

---

15 Meredith Broussard, *Artificial Unintelligence: How Computers Misunderstand the World* (Cambridge, MA: MIT Press, 2018), 89.

16 Not to mention the privacy implications of collecting all that data.

17 Merlin Mann, Twitter Post, April 15, 2011, 11:46am, https://twitter.com/hotdogsladies/status/58964552993357825.

newspapers, and other sources. With the exception of newspapers, most of the content is written without much thought of how it will be indexed in a search engine. Although Google Scholar does include many academic journals in its index, there aren't many academic authors (or journal editors) who are choosing specific keywords so that an academic article will appear higher up in particular search results. So we can be reasonably sure that the content indexed in our library discovery systems hasn't been written to "game" our discovery system's algorithm. (And since the market for library discovery is fairly diverse, it would be difficult to decide *which* algorithm to game. On the open web, nearly 80% of all searches go through some Google property,[18] so focusing your SEO on Google is a safe bet.)

These differences all contribute to making it easier (in some ways) to study the algorithmic outputs of library discovery than studying the outputs of Google searches. But there are other differences between horizontal search tools and library discovery that introduce new challenges, as well.

Perhaps the biggest challenge for studying the outputs of library discovery systems at scale is that the content that is returned to users from the index is entirely dependent on local collection practices. That is, my library discovery system will only show me results from my collection, not from the entire index.[19] While we can be confident that all users of our libraries' discovery system are seeing similar results, once we look at the same discovery system licensed by another library, the indexed content and algorithmic results will differ. Any attempt to examine the search outputs of a discovery system will need to be limited to a single institution, or else the complexity of collection development practices will need to be taken into account. Auxiliary algorithms like autosuggest and spelling correction are usually not

---

18   Net Market Share, "Search Engine Market Share."

19   Many discovery systems will allow users to see results from the index that are not included in their libraries' collection, but this is usually a filter that can be selected by a user on a search-by-search basis, rather than a default for all searches. See "Summon: Add Results Beyond Your Library's Collection," Ex Libris Knowledge Center, February 21, 2014, https://knowledge.exlibrisgroup.com/Summon/Product_Documentation/Searching_in_The_Summon_Service/Search_Features/Summon%3A_Add_Results_Beyond_Your_Library's_Collection, and "What is Available in Library Collection Limiter in EBSCO Discovery Service?," EBSCO, accessed January 17, 2019, https://help.ebsco.com/interfaces/EBSCO_Discovery_Service/EDS_FAQs/Available_in_Library_Collection_limiter_EDS.

affected by local practices, although some discovery systems like Summon allow individual licensing libraries to customize the sources for reference material in "Knowledge Graph-like" panels, as we will see in Chapter 5.

Because the content indexed in library discovery is provided by hundreds of different content providers who each have their own metadata standards, it can be a challenge to understand the reason that any particular result appears. Metadata such as author, title, dates, publisher, subject, and more are passed along in each publisher's format. This means that for any given date field, for instance, the discovery system may have to parse dozens of competing date formats. If you request items published in October of 2017, the discovery system will need to normalize all the content with dates that say "October 2017," "Oct. 17," 10/17," 10/2017," "19/10/17," and countless others.[20] One clear place where the messiness of discovery metadata leaks out into the interface is in the "Subject" facet of Summon's limiters. In Figure 3.1, Ex Libris shows exactly what subjects the publishers have provided to describe each item [Figure 3.1]. The exact same article, available through different providers, may have completely different metadata assigned to it. This is also complicated by the fact that subject terms may be terms assigned by authors and editors of a publication, or they may be terms assigned by an abstracting and indexing (A&I) service.[21] These library discovery tools do a decent job of parsing through this soup of metadata and making it intelligible. But for the most part, much of this metadata makes understanding the logic behind results more opaque than it might otherwise be.

To be fair, library discovery systems also have their own controlled vocabulary to help standardize this messy metadata. EBSCO has created a set of 70 "disciplines" that libraries can choose to show to users.[22] According to the help topic, disciplines appear to be assigned at the publication

---

20   Anyone who has ever had to troubleshoot OpenURL links provided by content aggregators that link to individual publisher sites, where date formats are used differently, will know how easy it is to lose content by changing the formatting of a single piece of metadata.

21   "What Is the Difference Between Subject Facets and Subject: Thesaurus Terms Facets?," EBSCO, accessed October 11, 2018, https://help.ebsco.com/interfaces/EBSCOhost/EBSCOhost_FAQs/difference_between_Subject_facets_and_Subject_Thesaurus_Terms_facets.

22   "EBSCO Discovery Service (EDS)—Discipline Limited Searching," EBSCO Connect, October 18, 2018, https://connect.ebsco.com/s/article/EBSCO-Discovery-Service-EDS-Discipline-Limited-Searching?language=en_US.

Figure 3.1 Screenshot of messy subject facet in Summon.

level, rather than the article level. So an interdisciplinary article published in a psychology journal would likely only appear when using the psychology discipline facet. Summon also has a discipline facet (in addition to the messy "Subject" facet described above). In their documentation, Ex Libris is very clear how they determine subjects:

> Using information from all of the sources, the Summon service maps Disciplines via the Subject Term and Call Number fields in the Summon index. Disciplines are mapped at the individual item-level, not at the broad database level. Journal articles, along with items from many other content types in Summon, have one or more Disciplines mapped to them.[23]

---

23   "Summon: Disciplines in the Summon Index," Ex Libris Knowledge Center, February 20, 2014, https://knowledge.exlibrisgroup.com/Summon/Product_Documentation/ Searching_in_The_Summon_Service/Search_Results/Summon%3A_Disciplines_in_ the_Summon_Index.

Ex Libris uses the Hierarchical Interface to Library of Congress Classification developed by Columbia University Library[24] to map subject terms from providers as well as subject terms in *Ulrich's*. They also use the Library of Congress Call Number, Dewey Number, or National Library of Medicine Classification to find subject terms.[25] This helps to provide some of the clarity that was leeched away by preserving and using provider subject terms, but continues to obscure how a discovery service's relevance algorithm chooses and ranks individual results.

Finally, a key difference between general purpose search engines and library discovery is in their respective End User License Agreements (EULAs). Since Google is effectively an advertising company, they want to get as many users as possible using their services. And so their EULA is fairly permissive when it comes to access.[26] They do include restrictions for automating queries, or using the tools for ways in which they were not intended, and library discovery services also have these restrictions. But EDS restricts access to its discovery system for many users. According to the EDS EULA, only "Authorized Users" can access the search tool, and:

> the "Authorized User(s)" are employees, students, registered patrons, walk-in patrons, or other persons affiliated with Licensee or otherwise permitted to use Licensee's facilities and authorized by Licensee to access Databases or Services.[27]

This means that libraries who license EDS are agreeing that only those affiliated with their institutions can use their online search tool. Often, EBSCO customers set up their EDS tool to require a user to log in before they can even run a search.[28] In order to allow public searching of the interface,

---

24 Stephen Paul Davis, "HILCC, A Hierarchical Interface to Library of Congress Classification," *Journal of Internet Cataloging* 5, no. 4 (2002): 19–49.

25 Ex Libris, "Summon: Disciplines in the Summon Index."

26 "Terms of Service," Google.com, April 16, 2007, https://tools.google.com/dlpage/res/webmmf/en/eula.html.

27 "EBSCO License Agreement," EBSCO, accessed February 12, 2019, https://www.ebsco.com/terms-of-use.

28 Or be on campus, which is a proxy for being a logged-in, affiliated user.

the licensing library must turn on a feature called "Guest Access." In my searching, I could only find a handful of libraries that had Guest Access turned on. But if you want to search across multiple platforms, you'll need to find a way to become an authorized user for an EDS instance in order to comply with the EULA. (Full disclosure: EBSCO generously provided me with my own EDS instance for my research in this book.)

OCLC's WorldCat Discovery and Ex Libris' Summon and Primo discovery services allow any user to use the search interface, but require credentials to access licensed content. In addition, some content is not visible in these search results unless the user is logged-in or on-campus, due to licensing restrictions. (This mostly affects A&I content.[29]) For the purposes of a study like this, OCLC and Ex Libris prohibit the use of scripts or other automated search tools, meaning that any comparative research must be done by typing searches one at a time into the search box.[30]

Despite all of these differences, one thing that library discovery systems and general purpose search engines agree on is cultivating an image of neutral objectivity. Grand Valley State University Libraries' Collection Strategist Angela Galvan notes that library discovery tools are intentionally designed to look like Google, mimicking the simple interface to suggest that the act of searching is also easy.[31] WorldCat Discovery boasts of its "authoritative e-content."[32] SirsiDynix, which doesn't currently have a horse in the discovery race but does promote its OPACs, emphasized in a marketing release entitled "Google vs. Library Databases: Which Is Better for Research?" that with library resources, "the authority and trustworthiness

---

29   Breeding, "Web-Scale Discovery Services."

30   "OCLC WorldCat.org Services Terms and Conditions," OCLC WorldCat, September 24, 2009, https://www.oclc.org/content/dam/ext-ref/worldcat-org/terms.html; "Primo Central Terms of Service," Ex Libris Knowledge Center, accessed February 12, 2019, https://knowledge.exlibrisgroup.com/Primo/Content_Corner/Product_Documentation/Primo_Central_Terms_of_Service; Ex Libris does not appear to have a Terms of Service document for Summon.

31   Angela Galvan, "Architecture of authority," December 5, 2016, https://asgalvan.com/2016/12/05/architecture-of-authority.

32   "Introduction to WorldCat Discovery," OCLC, December 23, 2018, https://help.oclc.org/Discovery_and_Reference/WorldCat_Discovery/Get_started/Introduction_to_WorldCat_Discovery_video.

of the articles don't need to be questioned."[33] At the same time, libraries around the world started creating their own "Library vs. Google" marketing materials. In one from a series of YouTube videos branded "University Library" (supposedly so any library could use them), the narrator states that "the University Library is the best resource for credible, peer-reviewed research" that is "academically sound."[34] The East Brunswick Public Library in New Jersey claims that "When you need accurate, reliable information," you should use the library, because "Google gives you the good with the bad, a mixture of trustworthy and not-so-trustworthy web sites."[35] The implication is that the library only gives you good, trustworthy information. There are examples of this at nearly every public and academic library I've looked at. If the libraries don't subscribe to a discovery system, then the authoritative marketing is moved to their subscription databases. The message all of these marketing efforts are aiming for is to take the trust we have in Google, and apply it to the library, with the additional claim that the library is even more trustworthy and objective than Google itself.

Examining the Trustworthiness of Library Search Algorithms

We've looked at commercial search engines' claims to trustworthiness, and there are many scholars examining this more closely.[36] For many of us, our interactions with commercial search engines reinforce the belief that they provide useful, trustworthy information for most searches. But as Noble and others have pointed out, search engines are best when retrieving information

---

33   Liz Van Halsema, "Google vs. Library Databases: Which is Better for Research?," SirsiDynix, September 29, 2014, http://www.sirsidynix.com/blog/2014/09/29/google-vs-library-databases-which-is-better-for-research.

34   libraryuopx, "Why the University Library Is Better Than Google for Research!," YouTube Video, 2:11, October 28, 2014, https://www.youtube.com/watch?v=G3yE2E-9z1o.

35   "Online Databases," East Brunswick Public Library, accessed October 14, 2018, https://www.ebpl.org/main/online_databases_info.cfm.

36   See also Noble, *Algorithms of Oppression*; Wachter-Boettcher, *Technically Wrong*; Hannah Fry, *Hello World: Being Human in the Age of Algorithms* (New York: W.W. Norton, 2018).

about the mundane business of everyday life.[37] Once you start to inquire about topics that are less straightforward, and therefore harder to represent in mathematical language, their usefulness and trustworthiness starts to decline.

But library discovery systems were designed specifically to deal with topics from the mundane to the complex, supporting the kinds of intellectual inquiry done at academic institutions across the world. Whereas commercial search tools rely on tracking users and personalization algorithms, library discovery systems generally do not personalize search results. A commercial search engine designed to handle a variety of tasks that can be mathematically modeled, such as "Find the nearest gas station" or "lowest price on a Honda Civic near me" can use location information to fill in the missing "near me" parts of the query, tailoring the results of identical searches to meet the needs of a user in Albuquerque and another in Hong Kong.

In addition, many commercial search tools also rely heavily on user search history and advertising profiling. Library discovery, on the other hand, will rarely show different results to different users of the same institution, although this doesn't mean that there aren't "personalization" options available in library discovery systems. Primo, for example, allows users to create a profile that includes their degrees and disciplines, and then allows the user to "personalize" search results on a search-by-search basis, which "boost the rankings of electronic records that match their preferred disciplines."[38] This is a fairly broad and crude form of personalization, one that mirrors work done by the University of Minnesota and others in the past, using discipline as a filter to show content that is assumed to be more

---

37 Ann Fisher, "All Sides with Ann Fisher: Tech Tuesday: Cybersecurity at the Olympics, Search Engine Bias," February 13, 2018, http://radio.wosu.org/post/tech-tuesday-cy-bersecurity-olympics-search-engine-bias#stream/0. At the 20:50 mark, Dr. Noble states: "The kinds of queries people present to search engines, you know if you're looking for where the closest Starbucks is, they might be perfectly fine. But when you start asking more complex questions about the meaning of things, this is where we get into a lot of trouble. And I think there are dire consequences over time for this."

38 "Personalizing Search Results in Primo VE," Ex Libris Knowledge Center, accessed February 12, 2019, https://knowledge.exlibrisgroup.com/Primo/Product_Documentation/020Primo_VE/100End_User_Help/015Personalizing_Search_Results_in_Primo_VE.

relevant.[39] Summon and EBSCO do not have any kind of "personalization" feature. And in all systems, the algorithms that help support the search process, like autosuggest, autocorrect, algorithms that expand your search based on thesaurus mapping (like Summon's query expansion), or results intended to familiarize the user with a broad topic, such as Google's Knowledge Graph, Summon's Topic Explorer, or EDS' Research Starters, are not affected by any form of personalization in library discovery.

The lack of individual personalization in library discovery has its roots in the professional ethics charters of organizations like the American Library Association (ALA), which values user privacy strongly.[40] Because commercial search tools are financially supported by advertising, the personalization algorithms are usually a derivative of the data collection done to serve relevant ads to various users. Since library discovery tools are not ad supported, and instead are paid for by licensing fees from individual libraries, the technological and ethical underpinnings of personalization are not present in library discovery tools.

Personalization also becomes a more sophisticated challenge for library discovery because of the varied collection development policies of each subscribing library. Because the discovery service only shows results

---

39   Cody Hanson, Shane Nackerud, and Kristi Jensen, "Affinity Strings: Enterprise Data for Resource Recommendations," *Code4Lib* 5 (December 15, 2008), https://journal.code4lib.org/articles/501.

40   "Professional Ethics," American Library Association, last modified January 22, 2008, http://www.ala.org/tools/ethics. Other countries do not share the same privacy emphasis as the ALA in the United States. For example, many European OPACs routinely keep a list of items you've checked out, and some discovery systems, like the University of Huddersfield's, can even track what articles you've looked at or recommend articles that other people who looked at this article have clicked on. See Dave Pattern, "Dumping the OPAC #2—usage Data," *Self Plagiarism is Style* (blog), May 25, 2013, https://www.daveyp.com/2013/05/25/dumping-the-opac-2-usage-data. Since the Patriot Act was passed in 2001 in the United States, many libraries configure their OPACs or other services to require users to opt-in to tracking services like this, and often do not even store records of which users have circulated particular materials. (The theory being that if the library doesn't have the records a law enforcement agency wants under the Act, they can't hand them over.) Of course, the increasing use of Google Analytics and the tendency to use identifying information about web content in the URL, coupled with universities increasingly moving to Google for email service, means that authorities could probably get even more information about a user's reading and search habits from asking Google for analytics data than they could from a library's Integrated Library System (ILS).

from the subset of its index that each subscribing library licenses, it is, in effect, already "personalizing" search results at the licensing library level.

Because the actual search results in a library discovery system vary from institution to institution, it is difficult to conduct a thorough analysis of the effectiveness of the main search algorithm. In order to do that, we'd need to have access to several different instances of each search tool and a way to compare the relevance of the various search results to the original search terms.

While the logistics for such a study could be arranged, it's usefulness is also dependent on the concept of "relevance." Every search tool promises to provide "relevant" results for its users, but what does this really mean? In many cases, the idea of relevance seems obvious. If I am using Google and I search for "restaurants near Grand Rapids, Michigan," relevant results would be restaurants in the geographic region I asked about. A restaurant in St. Petersburg, Florida, no matter how wonderful, is not a relevant result to this search. And when our searches are as mundane as looking for a restaurant by location or the best deal on a pair of sneakers, search algorithms are extremely adept at presenting relevant results. If the search itself can easily be reduced to an equation, then the algorithm has a good chance at working well. It's the kinds of searches that are not so easily reduced to right or wrong answers where relevance begins to be more complex.

You can modify our search above to show how dependent the search algorithm is on the specific keywords or other inputs for your search. If you simply searched for "restaurants," without specifying a specific geographic location, you might find that the results were not relevant to your need at all. In this case, you still want restaurants in the Grand Rapids area, but you neglected to tell the search engine about it. Most users would interpret this lack of relevant results as their own fault for not expressing all of the details of their information need. In fact, most search engines today will assume that a search for "restaurants" with no other parameters is one based on your current location. They will use your Internet Protocol (IP) address or other location information to tailor your search to your local area.

But when we move to academic search tools like library discovery we see this relevance problem in a new light. Because instead of searching for local restaurants, our users are searching for big, challenging, often contentious topics. There is no mathematically correct answer to a question about abortion rights or the death penalty. Yet libraries and vendors have promoted library discovery tools as effective guides through difficult subjects. But they were all designed with the assumption that an algorithm can infer everything relevant to a user from the keywords they enter into a search box. But this isn't always the case.

Let's look at a search for a contentious medical topic: fetal tissue research. Because library discovery systems do no individual personalization of the search results, all users of a particular institution will see the same results. Now let's imagine we have two different users who type this same search into the library's discovery tool. The first is a freshman economics major who was assigned a five-page paper in her writing class examining fetal tissue research from both the perspectives of proponents and opponents. Our other user is a tenured laboratory medical sciences professor who was just diagnosed with a rare form of cancer, and the oncologist told her that her best chance for treating the advanced nature of her disease was a form of fetal tissue therapy. Will these two users find the same results relevant to their information needs? It is unlikely. The freshman student is looking for broad overviews with which to construct a basic overview of two opposing positions, while the faculty member is looking for information that may save her life.

Of course, we could dispense with the dramatic situation our faculty member finds herself in and just ask whether a faculty member and a freshman will find the same results useful for their work in general. Again, it is unlikely that they will. Because the concept of relevant answers is entirely dependent on *who* is asking the question. As Gillespie noted,

> 'relevant' is a fluid and loaded judgment ... engineers must decide what looks 'right' and tweak their algorithm to attain that result ... or make changes based on evidence from their users, treating quick clicks and no follow-up searches as an approximation, not of relevance exactly, but of satisfaction.[41]

In simple questions, the for-whomness of the question can often be omitted or inferred, as in our geographically-specific example above. But when the questions become more dependent on the experience or expertise of the user, then the relevance of any possible answers becomes more tenuous. This also taps into the search engine's reputation as a trustworthy objective

---

41 Gillespie, "The Relevance of Algorithms," 175.

tool, as Noble points out, since "search results are not tied to a multiplicity of perspectives, and the epistemology of 'ranking' from one to a million or more sites suggests that what is listed first is likely to be the most credible and trustworthy information available."[42]

Any examination of the effectiveness of discovery algorithms then should focus on the "experience" algorithms that serve to improve the search experience or give context to users for a particular search. Autosuggest algorithms that show common searches as you type, query expansion or thesaurus algorithms ('also searching for' algorithms), and Knowledge Graph-style algorithms like Ex Libris' Topic Explorer or EBSCO's Research Starters show the same results to all users and show as few as one result each time, giving more weight to the "relevance" of each result.[43] In this study, I will focus on all of these auxilliary algorithms, but will pay special attention to the results generated by the Topic Explorer and Research Starters, since each algorithm only shows a single result. With only one result, the message to the user is simple: this is what you are searching for. And as we will see, the hubris inherent in the design and execution of such an algorithm will make for some unreliable, uncomfortable, and at times, offensive search results.

To begin the study, it would help to understand the infrastructure that underlies these experience algorithms. This is a challenge, however, because these algorithms are black-boxed. By sharing the specific details of how these algorithms are constructed and how they make decisions, discovery providers would lose a perceived advantage in the competitive marketplace. After all, library discovery is a zero-sum game: no library subscribes

---

42 Noble, *Algorithms of Oppression*, 118.

43 In the case of Summon, each instance of Summon has the option of selecting the sources for the Topic Explorer, and many of these are dependent on local collection practices. Institutions that do not subscribe to Credo Reference can use the Gale Virtual Reference Library, World Book, Encyclopedia Britannica, or JapanKnowledge. "Summon Topics," Ex Libris Knowldge Center, accessed February 12, 2019, https://knowledge.exlibrisgroup.com/Summon/Product_Documentation/Searching_in_The_Summon_Service/Search_Results/Summon%3A_Summon_Topics. Wikipedia, however, is the most common source and is turned on by default on all new installations.

to more than one discovery system.[44] And since a discovery system often works best with the vendors' other products, such as subscription databases and journals, link resolvers, Integrated Library Systems (ILS), Electronic Resources Management Systems (ERMS), and other administrative apparatus, the economic advantage of making a case for a better discovery system can easily capture hundreds of thousands of dollars a year for a vendor from a single academic library in licensing fees.

But while these vendors have chosen not to share the details of how they create their algorithms or which factors are weighed in precisely what amounts each time a search is done, there are ways that we can examine the tools to better understand some of the assumptions that went into its development, and perhaps what sorts of decisions are made each time a search is done. After all, these search tool algorithms all produce visible outputs in the form of search results. By carefully calibrating our searches and examining the different results, as well as carefully reading the documentation and release notes, we can start to get a sense of how these discovery systems make their decisions. This method is probably more effective for understanding the algorithmic makeup of a search tool than looking at the actual code by itself, as anyone who has ever read someone else's code can tell you. The code itself will not show us the assumptions that went into writing the methods and functions, and a complex search tool like a discovery system likely has so many steps and factors that it is unlikely that any single developer who works on the system understands the algorithm completely, let alone an outside auditor examining just the code base. Even if we had access to the code behind these search tools, we wouldn't be able to make heads or tails out of what was happening without doing some testing of inputs and outputs.

As I progress through this study, I will bring up relevant techniques for understanding the workings of the algorithms through careful audits, examining the release notes and documentation, and flat out asking the project managers or developers. But to examine how much we can learn from these pragmatic techniques, I will share one example of investigating a

---

44   There have been a few libraries that have had two systems installed at the same time, either because they were comparing the two in anticipation of subscribing to a discovery system for the first time, or phasing out one in favor of the other. See, for instance, Andrew Asher, Lynda M. Duke, and Suzanne Wilson, "Paths of Discovery: Comparing the Search Effectiveness of EBSCO Discovery Service, Summon, Google Scholar, and Conventional Library Resources," *College and Research Libraries* 74, no. 5 (2013): 464–83.

search algorithm's outputs strategically in order to better understand the assumptions and architecture behind it. Let's look at how Summon integrated Wikipedia results into its Topic Explorer algorithm.

In May of 2018, Ruth Kitchin Tillman, the Cataloging Systems & Linked Data Strategist at Penn State University Libraries, emailed me about some problematic results she had found in Summon's Topic Explorer algorithm. We had shared problematic Topic Explorer results before when I was initially doing research a few years earlier on bias in the Topic Explorer. This time, however, rather than biased results, she had written to share some factual errors on Topic Explorer results that claimed to be coming from Wikipedia. The first result was a search for Barack Obama, the former President of the United States. The Wikipedia entry displayed on the Summon search, seen in Figure 3.2, said that Barack Obama is "the 44th and current president of the United States of America." The problem was that Barack Obama left office in January of 2017 when Donald Trump was inaugurated as the 45th president. Nearly a year-and-a-half after he left office, the Wikipedia entry shown in Summon was still saying that Barack Obama was president. A quick visit to the Wikipedia website showed that the current entry for Barack Obama correctly stated that he was the former president. This was such a basic, verifiable fact that it seemed like an anomaly for it to be wrong.

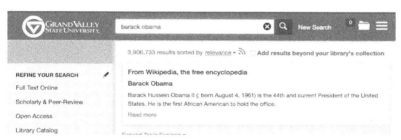

Figure 3.2 Summon Topic Explorer showing Barack Obama as current president, 18 months after he left office.

Yet Ruth also sent me the results for a search for Donald Trump, shown in Figure 3.3, which indicated that he was merely a reality television star and real estate mogul. It did not mention any political experience, despite the fact that he had been serving as the president of the United States for a year and a half. Presented with these factually incorrect results, Penn State turned off the Topic Explorer in the sidebar in July of 2018. At Grand Valley, however, our Topic Explorer was still running, and I was curious about the cause of these issues. The Wikipedia entries for both men were likely edited in the very same minute that Donald Trump took the oath of office to reflect the new political reality in the U.S. Why had it taken Summon so long to get the updated information into its results?

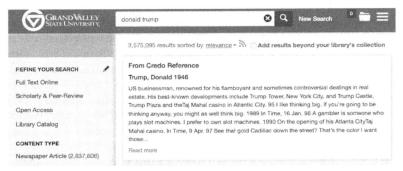

Figure 3.3 Summon Topic Explorer showing Donald Trump, leaving out the Presidency.

I started with a fairly obvious hypothesis: Summon was clearly not using the Wikipedia Application Programming Interface (API). An API is a way for programmers and applications to get data out of one system into another. In this case, Wikipedia provides an API so that developers can build Wikipedia into their own apps, like Summon. But if Summon was using the Wikipedia API, it would be returning the most current results, not results that were a year out of date. And so I started doing some more searching. Along with my hypothesis about Summon not using the API, I realized that these kinds of factual issues were more likely to happen with entries about people, rather than entries about broad subjects. After all, the lives of people change frequently. Politicians leave office, authors release new books, and people get married, divorced, or die. I decided to do a very basic audit, running a number of searches in Summon for famous individuals who were likely to have Wikipedia entries. Then I would be able see how widespread these inaccuracies went.

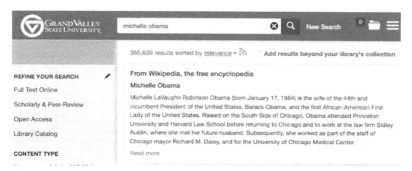

Figure 3.4   Summon Topic Explorer showing Michelle Obama, incorrectly listing her as the current First Lady of the United States in late 2018.

I found that Summon also said that Michelle Obama was still the first lady of the United States (Figure 3.4). I ran several searches for media personalities, but while these individuals had Wikipedia pages, they did not have Topic Explorer entries in Summon. This told me that the Summon team was limiting the number of items from Wikipedia that were showing up in the Topic Explorer, and entries for individuals that were part of "pop culture" didn't seem as likely to appear as entries for politicians, authors, or individuals who were more likely to be studied at the kinds of institutions that would subscribe to a library discovery system.[45] Right away I was confronted with what appeared to be an assumption about how library patrons will use a discovery system: not for searching for information about pop culture icons (except, perhaps those that are deceased), but for searches on "academic" topics. I recalibrated my list of potential search topics and started over.

According to Summon's Topic Explorer, Barbara Bush was alive and well, even though she had died a month before my search. I was starting to see a pattern here, with only four results. All were results of people, and all were out of date, even though each entry was no more than 3 sentences long. I continued to find additional inaccuracies: the writer Phillip Roth, according to Summon, was still alive. But, like Barbara Bush, he had died

---

45   Yes, I know that there are thriving areas of research throughout the humanities in particular into pop culture. But do the software developers who create library discovery tools know that? It doesn't appear so.

in 2018. Then I saw that Summon also thought that Christopher Lee, the British actor, was alive (Figure 3.5). He died in 2015, over three years before I was running these searches. Perhaps these inaccuracies went back farther than I had imagined? Could it be that there were no regular updates of the Wikipedia entries?

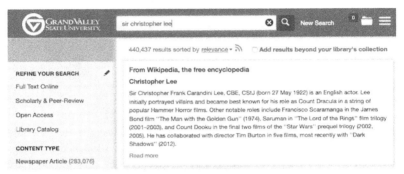

Figure 3.5   Summon Topic Explorer entry showing Christopher Lee alive, three years after he died.

I began to use Wikipedia's history feature to trace when edits were made to individual entries. Christopher Lee's entry was edited to reflect his death on June 11th, four days after he died but the same day it was publicly announced.[46] Yet three years later, Summon was still showing the actor to be alive. For a library to offer a tool that is said to be trustworthy, and to have that tool show such profound mistakes was a real problem. But I was also starting to understand some of the assumptions that the developers made when creating the Topic Explorer.

At this point, I was fairly certain that the Summon team had ingested the Wikipedia content that they wanted to use into the Summon index. Since using the Wikipedia API would have left the actual matching algorithms up to the Wikipedia team, the Summon team likely wanted to have more control over which results actually showed up on the Summon

---

46   "Christopher Lee: History," *Wikipedia,* June 11, 2015, https://en.wikipedia.org/w/index.php?title=Christopher_Lee&oldid=666471973.

interface, and so they wanted to use their own relevance algorithms, and thus, their own index. To understand this, I have to back up and explain how a search engine index works. While there are variations on the structures of these indexes, it's important to understand how content is ingested into the index and how search engines use these indexes to return results when a user submits a search.

First, a search engine scans the content it wants to add to its index. In the case of Google, this would be a web page, or in the case of library discovery, it might be an eBook, a catalog record, or a PDF of an article. Rather than storing an exact copy of the page as part of the search process, search engines instead make a sort of map of the content on the page. It will look at each word on the page and save its location. So, for instance, if a search engine is indexing an eight-paragraph article on skin grafting technology, and the second paragraph begins with the phrase "Skin grafting is a new technology," the search engine will add to its index some way to find the exact location of those words. For our simplified example, let's say that it counts the words in an article, and assigns each word its place. So, if the first paragraph of the article in question is 178 words long, the opening sentence of paragraph two would begin by indexing word number 179, "Skin." It would add this phrase in a way similar to that in Figure 3.6:

Position	Word
179	skin
180	grafting
181	is
182	a
183	new
184	technology

Figure 3.6   Sample index table for hypothetical search engine.

The reason to break the content up in this way is that computers can look up small bits of information in a database much more quickly than they could scan through all the content of the pages. Our example is extremely simple, but in reality the search engine index will have several tables. This will allow them to have, for instance, a table of all the words in a particular language. Each word would have a unique identifier. Then they would have another table that connected all the occurrences of each of those words with the page table. So each time the word "skin" appeared, there would be a reference to both the web page or article it appears in and the word table. In Figure 3.7 below, the unique identifier for the word "skin" is 17687. Now, instead of scanning through all the text of everything in its index, a search engine will instead take a search for the word "skin," look it up in the word table, and then ask to also see all of the entries in the second table with the unique identifier of 17687. It doesn't necessarily need to know in what context the word "skin" appears (yet), it just needs to know that the word is there.

Word Table

Word ID	Word
17687	Skin

Word Index

Word ID	Page ID	Position
17687	11	45
17687	19	414
17687	213	178

Pages

Page ID	URL	Title
11	https://skingrafting.com/index.html	Skin Grafting
19	http://skininfo.org/index.html	Skin Info : Home
213	http://dermotology.info/skingraft.html	Skin Grafting Information

Figure 3.7   Sample index tables for hypothetical search engine.

But this simple example of a search index will start to stumble quickly, especially when doing a search on academic topics. Take the search term "stress." As I discussed in Chapter 1, stress is a term used in everyday life, as well as a technical term used in both the social sciences (in much the same way we use it in daily life) as well as in engineering. For a structural engineer, stress has a very different meaning than it would have for a psychologist. Since our simple search engine is only looking at whether a word appears in an article or web page and ignoring the use of the word or its context, our current search engine is potentially going to return a lot of documents about bridge design to someone who is feeling overwhelmed at work. The search index needs a way to evaluate the context of the search terms to better understand what the user needs.

Because we were careful to record the position of the word on the page, rather than just the URL, we have a simple way to examine the context of the search. We look at all the words the user types into the search, and look for all of them in the index. But rather than just returning every example of the word stress, we can also look to see if the other words our user has searched for appear close to the word "stress" in any of the documents. This is called word proximity, and it is a proxy for context.

If we search now for "stress in the workplace," our search index doesn't need to understand that the word "workplace" is a hint that we do not want any engineering texts. By looking at word proximity only, we can do a fairly decent job of finding results that have the words "stress" and "workplace" in them, but prioritize the results that have these two words fairly close together. (If we had included these terms in quotes, we would force the search index to only return results for the exact phrase we searched for, which is a bit limiting. All modern search tools have some way of factoring word proximity into their relevance algorithms. Summon even lets you specify your own parameters for word proximity.[47]) So while Summon may return a million or more results for a search like "stress in the workplace," and many of them *may* be about engineering, they will probably be so far down the list of possible results that the

---

47 "Summon: Phrase, Field, Boolean, Wildcard and Proximity Searching," Ex Libris Knowledge Center, March 24, 2014, https://knowledge.exlibrisgroup. com/Summon/Product_Documentation/Searching_in_The_Summon_Service/ Search_Features/Summon%3A_Boolean%2C_Phrase%2C_Wildcard_and_Proximity_Searching.

results that have the words "stress" and "workplace" close together will crowd them out.[48]

By building a search index, the developers of a search tool can have more control over how their tool selects results. In the case of Summon and the Topic Explorer, they chose to ingest all of the Wikipedia content they wanted into the index so that they would be able to train their word proximity algorithms on the indexed content, rather than relying on the results that Wikipedia's APIs would provide. By relying on the API, they would be constrained by Wikipedia's search index, and their algorithms for choosing relevant results.

When I first began researching Summon's Topic Explorer algorithms, when I would encounter problematic results in the Topic Explorer I would often run our user's search directly on Wikipedia's site to see how different the results would have been had Summon been pulling directly from the Wikipedia API.[49] In many cases, I found that what appeared in Summon to be an incorrect or biased result from Wikipedia would have been better served by a more appropriate article in Wikipedia. And using the same search terms as our users, Wikipedia often returned these more appropriate results. So, in making the technical choice during the development of Summon 2.0 and the Topic Explorer algorithm, the developers had chosen the

---

48   Even if a discovery service returns a million results, the vast majority of them may be unavailable to users. In the case of Summon, only the first 200 results will be shown. Institutions can move that up to 1000, but the default behavior is to stop showing results after 200. This is because user research shows that the vast majority of people do not look at more than a few dozen results. According to Ex Libris, "less than 0.25% (a quarter of one percent) of searches go beyond 150 results and even fewer reach 200." See "Summon: Record Contents and Display," Ex Libris Knowledge Center, August 15, 2016, https://knowledge.exlibrisgroup.com/Summon/Product_Documentation/Searching_in_The_Summon_Service/Search_Results/Summon%3A_Record_Contents_and_Display.). In my own research collecting anonymized click data in Summon, over half of the clicks were on the top three or four results. Dave Pattern of the University of Huddersfield found a similar result on their usage. See Dave Pattern, "Relevance Rules," *Self Plagiarism is Style* (blog), May 6, 2012, https://www.daveyp.com/2012/05/06/relevancy-rules/. It also helps relieve load on the servers, and helps Ex Libris comply with restrictive licensing agreements from content providers. See Ex Libris, "Summon: Record Contents and Display."

49   I was using the public user interface, and not the API. It is possible that the Wikipedia API returns different results than the public interface, but since Wikipedia aims to have its content included in as many places as possible, it would be in its best interest to return the same results for everyone to ensure consistency and build trust.

convenience of their own relevance algorithm over Wikipedia's algorithms. Keep in mind that Summon's algorithms are very generalized, designed to index and return results from a variety of different formats, providers, authors, and metadata schemas. Wikipedia, on the other hand, has a robust set of guidelines for structuring results.[50] Authors ensure that the formatting guidelines are followed and that content is accurate. Because Wikipedia's relevance algorithms are written to only search Wikipedia content, it is plausible that their relevance algorithms will be better suited for returning relevant results from Wikipedia entries than a more generalized index designed for academic articles.

These kinds of choices in the architecture and development of software are almost never made public. In some cases, it may not even occur to the development team what the implications are for making these choices. This was likely the case with Summon's decision to ingest the Wikipedia content into its own index.

The fact that Summon's Wikipdia content wasn't up to date was especially strange, because Summon has a built-in feature for clients to upload content that is rapidly changing in the index: the individual holdings of each licensing library. Every time a library buys a book, discards a book, adds a subscription database or journal, or changes the location of an item, the content needs to be updated in the Summon index. Subscribers upload change files regularly to Summon, often daily, to ensure that their holdings are accurately reflected in the search results. While it is certainly possible that the Summon team had planned to update the Wikipedia content more regularly, it is also possible that they designed the system to not have a way to update the content of the Topic Explorer for Wikipedia entries. As I continued to search for various authors and politicians, I came across an entry that confirmed another suspicion I had: that the Wikipedia content had been added to the index and never updated.

Chris Ware is a well-known cartoonist who has reinvented the medium of comics with his sharp lines, complex compositions, and non-linear storytelling. Chris Ware's entry in Summon's Topic Explorer, provided by Wikipedia, lists his genre-changing works as his long-running series *The Acme Novelty Library* and *Jimmy Corrigan: The Smartest Kid on Earth.*

---

50   "Article Development," *Wikipedia*, March 9, 2018, https://en.wikipedia.org/wiki/Wikipedia:Article_development.

Figure 3.8   Summon Topic Explorer entry showing Chris Ware's Wikipedia history entry.

But a visit to the current Wikipedia page also lists another work, one that brought Ware even more acclaim and new audiences: the non-linear *Building Stories*, which was published in 2012. By examining the History tab of Chris Ware's Wikipedia page, I saw that on February 18th, 2013, the initial sentence in the page was edited to include *Building Stories* (Figure 3.8). The entry in Summon does not have this addition, which means that the Wikipedia content in Summon hasn't been updated since before February 18, 2013. It is unnecessary to continue to go back further, because the press release announcing Summon 2.0 came out March 20, 2013, a full month later. This means that for the entire life of Summon 2.0 and the Topic Explorer, the Wikipedia content has been frozen with information written before the product was actually available to libraries. (I was a member of the Summon 2.0 library advisory team, and the lack of an update strategy was never mentioned. From my notes I was under the impression that this content was being retrieved by API, but there has never been a public comment from the Summon team about this.) This tool, which is marketed as a way to solidify trust in library content and compete with Google, was serving up outdated articles and passing them off as current, credible facts, using the Wikipedia name to imply that the content was at the very least up-to-date. But the developers never updated the content, as if it never occurred to them that our knowledge about something changes over time, that information about people must evolve to keep up with the circumstances of their lives. When I asked the Summon project manager Brett Cook about this issue, he indicated that they hadn't foreseen the lack of updates as a problem. "It's a sad day when print encyclopedias are more up to date than your digital entries," he said.[51]

The developers of Summon made specific assumptions about the nature of knowledge as they were designing their discovery interface. They assumed that broad topics can easily be identified from a few keywords, and reference material is always a reliable knowledge source. Ironically, their view of the reliability of reference material may have actually been shaped by Wikipedia's constantly-evolving content. Because Wikipedia's entries reflect the deaths of celebrities moments after they die, and include information from breaking news accounts, the idea of reference sources as reliable information for all topics has become the norm. But print encyclopedias have had issues with accuracy surrounding biographical information since the form was invented. Beginning in 1910, the Encyclopaedia Britannica began including biographies of living persons,[52] but the medium made it clear that newer editions would by necessity update the entries. In ingesting Wikipedia's content into the Summon index, the discovery system's developers removed the innovative part of Wikipedia, what set it apart from the print reference material of the past. In effect, they fixed Wikipedia entries in early 2013, as if they had been printed and bound. Of course, this put Wikipedia in the same boat as subscription reference sources like Credo Reference or Gale Virtual Reference Library, which are only updated when the reference materials they aggregate update their content, or, in some cases, when an institution pays to update their content content.[53]

Early in my research into the Topic Explorer, Grand Valley was using the Gale Virtual Reference Library (GVRL) as a secondary source to

---

51 Brent Cook (Summon Project Manager, Ex Libris), email message to author, May 31, 2018.

52 "Encyclopædia Britannica: Print Encyclopaedia," Encyclopædia Britannica, accessed October 13, 2018, https://www.britannica.com/topic/Encyclopaedia-Britannica-print-encyclopaedia.

53 Credo and Gale Virtual Reference Library offer "one-time purchase" packages that do not include updates, as the subscription-based models do. But even the subscription-based models only update when the aggregated content is updated.

supplement content from Wikipedia. GVRL had several problems in this capacity, the most obvious being that the articles were clearly written for a print publication, and not for a service that would serve up the first paragraph of content as a "summary." Wikipedia has robust content creation guidelines, which direct its authors to start each entry with a few sentence overview, and then work into more details as the article progresses.[54] In journalism this method of writing is referred to as the "inverted pyramid" method—where your content is very broad at the beginning, like the base of an upside-down pyramid, and then as you move into the article, the content becomes more focused. Wikipedia uses this structure because they have specifically designed their content to be used in many different contexts. You can simply pull the summary section of an entry from the Wikipedia API to give a quick summary of a topic, and this way Wikipedia does not need to ensure that there is a separate summary written of the entire entry. They know that the first paragraph is already written as a summary.

The content in Credo Reference and GVRL is not this way. The authors were not encouraged to write based on the inverted pyramid. Instead, these entries are written by subject-area experts who are writing under the assumption that their work will appear in print and that readers will start at the beginning and then read the entire essay. So when the Summon team decided to pull a "summary" of each entry from these providers, they made the assumption that the content was created in the same way as Wikipedia—that it was designed to be reused. The result is Topic Explorer entries like the one in Figure 3.9 below. There is no useful information in this entry for anyone searching for information about art.

The other issue is related to the problems of accuracy and recency we saw in examining Wikipedia. The content in Credo and GVRL is rarely updated. If you search in Summon in 2018 for Osama bin Laden, the Credo Reference (or GVRL) entry will tell you that he is still alive and leading al Queda. There is no mention that Osama bin Laden was assassinated by the United States in 2011, over 8 years ago. This is because the entry for Osama bin Laden available to GVSU in Credo Reference, shown in Figure 3.10, was written in the Fall of 2002, just one year after September 11th.

And this is not related only to Summon. EDS, which relies also on encyclopedia articles written by experts, is vulnerable to the same inaccuracies.

---

54   "Article Development," Wikipedia.

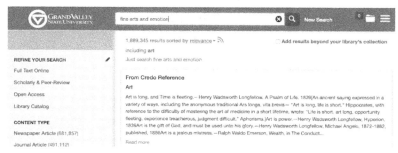

Figure 3.9 Credo entry for 'Art,' which appears to be a collection of disjointed quotes.

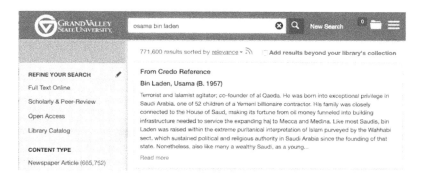

Figure 3.10 Summon Topic Explorer showing Credo Reference Entry for Osama bin Laden

In September of 2018, the Research Starter for "Donald Trump" was written in 2015, before he announced his candidacy for President. Now, after serving 21 months as President, EDS still does not mention this aspect of his biography. (Although as you can see in Figure 3.11, below the main entry are the related topics, which point you to the 2016 Presidential election, the Trump Organization, and the entry for "President.")

The point here is not that Wikipedia is a bad source for discovery systems, or that we shouldn't invest in reference content like Credo or Gale Virtual Reference Library. The point here is that the assumptions we make about the things we design, build, purchase, and subscribe to need to be examined closely. The Summon and EDS teams made a lot of assumptions about how their Topic Explorer and Research Starters would be used, but

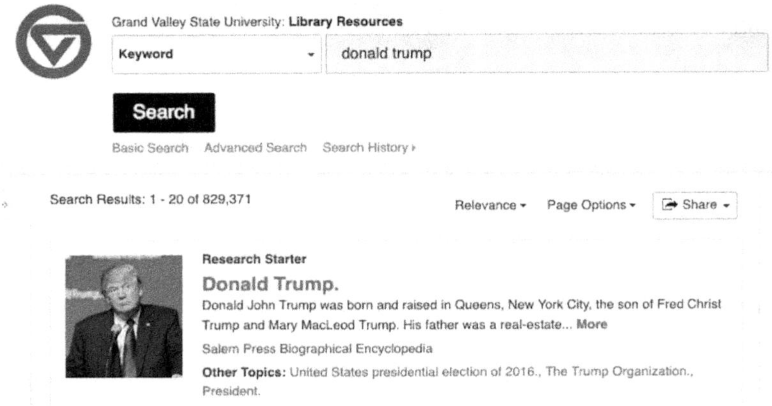

Figure 3.11   Donald Trump Research Starter in EDS

failed to see the danger in showing "authoritative" content that is never up-dated. Libraries continue to assume that content delivered digitally is more up-to-date than print material. Credo Reference and GVRL show us that this is definitely not the case. (In fact, much of this material is the same content libraries purchased in print a decade ago, just scanned and resold to us.)

Here, the unexamined assumptions of software developers and librarians have led to incorrect and, frankly, embarrassing content being displayed in the very tools we claim are more objective and reliable than Google. But this is only scratching the surface of the problems created by building search tools on unexamined assumptions. As Noble said,

> When we inherit privilege, it is based on a massive knowledge regime that foregrounds the structural inequalities of the past, buttressed by vast stores of texts, images, and sounds saved in archives, museums, and libraries. ... In the case of most library databases in the United States, Eurocentrism will dominate the canons of knowledge. Knowledge management reflects the same social biases that exist in society, because human beings are at the epicenter of information curation.[55]

---

55   Noble, *Algorithms of Oppression*, 140–41.

In the context of our examination of the Topic Explorer, what Noble is pointing to is that the social bias inherent in the way white, male westerners see the world will necessarily bleed through into any system that they create. Therefore, Topic Explorer results will skew towards Eurocentric topics (Summon only provides topics in non-English languages from two sources: JapanKnowledge and Wikipedia.[56]) The software developers behind these discovery systems assumed that the very knowledge they were tapping to build their search tools was unbiased and objective. What they didn't realize is that the very act of curation itself, something necessary to the work of librarians, archivists, and scholars who have built up the body of knowledge that they are working with, reflect the same deep-rooted social biases about race, gender, ethnicity, sexual orientation, religion, and more. By glossing over these ingrained biases, the software developers have created a search tool for finding not only incorrect information, but for finding biased information.

---

56   Ex Libris, "Summon Topics."

Chapter 4   What is Bias?

In looking at the effectiveness of Summon's Topic Explorer algorithm, we saw problems with the accuracy of some results it returned. But at times, incorrect results can feel like they have moved from being factually wrong to being biased. Bias can appear in many ways, and can come from many sources. But when supposedly objective search results reflect the kinds of structural inequalities that we struggle with in our daily lives like racism and sexism, there is a good chance that these systemic biases have crept into the algorithms behind search. As Dormehl reminds us, because technology aims not to describe but to change the world, it is "a discipline that is inextricably tied in with a sense of morality regardless of how much certain individuals might try to deny it."[1] According to Mittelstadt et al, "algorithms are inescapably value-laden."[2] The values held by the company, the designers, the software developers, the venture capitalists, and the shareholders will necessarily affect the final product, and often these values are not made explicit during the process of creating algorithmic systems. More than just a problem for the algorithmic code, these values will come into play in the outputs of the algorithm, and necessarily shape the lives of those who depend on those outputs. As Greenfield wrote about algorithms, "whatever values and priorities are inscribed in it [an algorithm] will be incorporated

---

1   Dormehl, *The Formula*, 132.

2   Mittelstadt et al., "The Ethics of Algorithms," 1.

by reference into everything it touches."[3] Even those at the forefront of creating these tools are aware of bias in the development process. According to Veronica Vargas, a consultant for IBM, "there are no computer systems that are without human bias."[4]

Mike Ananny, an Associate Professor of Communication and Journalism at the Annenberg School for Communication and Journalism at the University of Southern California, wrote of installing Grindr, a location-based dating and socializing app for gay men, and looking at the algorithmically generated "related" apps. Included was a "Sex Offender Search" app. In teasing out how the algorithm decided that gay men and sex offenders were topically related, he notes that "reckless associations—made by humans or computers—can do very real harm especially when they appear in supposedly neutral environments."[5] In 2013, Latanya Sweeney, Professor of Government and Technology in Residence and the Director of the Data Privacy Lab in the Institute of Quantitative Social Science (IQSS) at Harvard University, published an article that argued that searching for "racially associated" names on Google and other services had a significant effect on whether you were shown an advertisement implying that the person you were searching for had been arrested. "Black-identifying names" like De-Shawn and Trevon were 25% more likely to be shown an ad suggesting that the person had been arrested than names associated with whites, like Jill or Emma. These results are not connected to whether the names actually have an arrest record, but seem to be algorithmically biased.[6] These results reflect the systemic racial, gender, and anti-gay biases that have bled over into many facets of our society. It is more than just "wrong" to show arrest advertisements more for "black sounding names" than white ones, it is racist. And linking sex offenders to gay men digs up common tropes used by anti-gay conservatives that have been in use for generations.

---

3 Greenfield, *Radical Technologies,* 275.

4 Lohr, *Data-ism,* 160.

5 Mike Ananny, "The Curious Connection Between Apps for Gay Men Ad Sex Offenders," *The Atlantic,* April 14, 2011, https://www.theatlantic.com/technology/archive/2011/04/the-curious-connection-between-apps-for-gay-men-and-sex-offenders/237340/.

6 Latanya Sweeney, "Discrimination in online ad delivery," *Communications of the ACM* 56, no. 5 (2013): 44–54.

These technology companies have promised us a better world, but in this they have failed. As Broussard notes, this "is the same world with the same types of human problems that have always existed. The problems are hidden inside code and data, which makes them harder to see and easier to ignore."[7] But how did these results end up in these algorithmic systems? Were they explicitly programmed to be racist, to be homophobic? This is not likely. Rather, in this chapter I will explore many of the factors that lead algorithms to show biased results.

The study of bias in search results has a long history. In 2002, the computer science professors from City College of New York Abbe Mowshowitz and Akira Kawaguchi emphasized the need for this kind of analysis, since "the role played by retrieval systems as gateways to information coupled with the absence of mechanisms to insure fairness makes bias in such systems an important social issue." For them, bias "deliberately provides an unbalanced picture of its subjects,"[8] but, we will see, much of the bias that we find in results is likely not deliberate on the part of the search engine companies.

Mowshowitz and Kawaguchi focused primarily on the difference between what they called "indexical bias," where the juxtaposition of two terms or ideas can suggest bias—and "content bias," where the content itself contains biased information.[9] Indeed, many such studies have looked for anomalies in results. According to a group of researchers studying perceptions of Facebook's News Feed, "researchers have paid particular attention to algorithms when outputs are unexpected or when the risk exists that the algorithm might promote antisocial political, economic, geographic, racial, or other discrimination."[10] Because the workings of these algorithmic systems are "black boxes," Associate Professor of Internet Studies at Curtin University Michele Willson notes that it is harder for everyday users

---

7   Broussard, *Artificial Unintelligence,* 194.

8   Abbe Mowshowitz and Akira Kawaguchi, "Assessing Bias in Search Engines," *Information Processing and Management* 38, no. 1 (2013): 143.

9   Mowshowitz and Kawaguchi, 143.

10   Motahhare Eslami et al., "'I Always Assumed That I Wasn't Really Close to [Her]': Reasoning About Invisible Algorithms in News Feeds," *33rd Annual ACM Conference on Human Factors in Computing Systems,* (2015), 154.

and researchers to understand how and why algorithms work the way they do. As a result, "unintended and unanticipated consequences are an obvious, and will be an increasingly common, outcome."[11] Yet these problematic, and at times biased, results are often seen not as problems, but as truths emerging out of data.

The marketing of the objectivity of algorithms over people has been so thorough, and the pressures of computer science so great, that these conditions encourage software creators to "obscure the role of human beings in creating technological systems or training data."[12] But Kitchin reminds us that not only are algorithms themselves "not neutral, impartial expressions of knowledge," but

> their work is not impassive and apolitical [either]. Algorithms search, collate, sort, categorize, group, match, analyse, profile, model, simulate, visualise and regulate people, processes and places. They shape how we understand the world and they do work in and make the world through their execution as software, with profound consequences.[13]

That is, while much of the popular focus on bias in algorithms has focused on the code and how bias could have been mistakenly programmed in (or overlooked in a training data set in the case of machine learning algorithms), Kitchin reminds us that algorithms gain power through their work on the world. The idea that algorithms are objective also plays into the impact they have, notes David Beer, professor of sociology at York University.[14] They have real consequences in our daily lives, and so bias impacts us as we live our lives, often without us being aware that an algorithm has made biased choices for us.

In the *New York Times*, Jody Kantor wrote about the impact that algorithmic scheduling software has had on workers, particularly those in

---

11   Michele Willson, "Algorithms (And The) Everyday," *Information, Communication & Society* 20, no. 1 (2017): 144.

12   Broussard, *Artificial Unintelligence,* 199.

13   Kitchin, "Thinking Critically About and Researching Algorithms," 18.

14   David Beer, "The Social Power of Algorithms," *Information, Communication & Society* 20, no. 1 (2017): 2.

the service sector that already lack many of the amenities of profession-al-class jobs, like steady work schedules, a living wage, and benefits such as health insurance. Most major companies, like Starbucks, use software to schedule workers "using sales patterns and other data to determine which of its 130,000 baristas are needed in its thousands of locations and exactly when."[15] Jannette Navarro, a single mother who works for Starbucks, notes that the software dictated "how much sleep Gavin [her son] will get to what groceries I'll be able to buy this month."[16]

Eubanks has also studied the effects of algorithms in controlling the daily lives of people. She notes that the lives of the homeless and poor are increasingly controlled by algorithmic systems. These systems are based on models of the world that may not reflect the values of the poor and home-less people whose lives are affected. For instance, one algorithm that helps predict a homeless person's chances of being helped by social services (the VI-SPDAT) asks about recent housing. The creators of the tool decided that prison would count as housing, affecting the scores of anyone who had been incarcerated.[17] Eubanks notes that for many of these projects, and indeed algorithmic systems in general, the creators "refused to anticipate or address the system's human costs."[18] In fact, "this myopic focus on what's new leads us to miss the important ways that digital tools are embedded in old sys-tems of power and privilege ... It is mere fantasy to think that a statistical model or a ranking algorithm will magically upend culture, policies, and institutions built over centuries."[19]

These are examples of algorithms controlling the lives of poor and working class people, but algorithms do not stop there. (Although O'Neil notes that the poor are processed more by algorithms than those who have more.[20]) Algorithms are, as Beer has said, "a powerful if largely unnoticed

---

15 Jody Kantor, "Working Anything but 9 to 5: Scheduling Technology Leaves Low-In-come Parents With Hours of Chaos," *New York Times,* August 13, 2014, https://www.nytimes.com/interactive/2014/08/13/us/starbucks-workers-scheduling-hours.html.

16 Kantor.

17 Eubanks, *Automating Inequality,* 126.

18 Eubanks, 75.

19 Eubanks, 178.

20 O'Neil, *Weapons of Math Destruction,* 8.

social presence."[21] Writing about New York City's proposal to make the algorithms that help city government more accountable, journalist Julia Powles noted that a few of the ways that algorithms affect the daily lives of New Yorkers were "matching students with schools, assessing teacher performance, rooting out Medicaid fraud, and helping building inspectors manage their workloads."[22] O'Neil notes that "algorithms choose the information we see when we go online, the jobs we get, the colleges to which we're admitted and the credit cards and insurance we are issued."[23] Dwyer reminds us that algorithms also determine "how often garbage is picked up, [and] which police precincts get the most officers."[24] Algorithms are being created to help determine whether a crime was gang related,[25] what nationality and ethnicity you are based only on your name,[26] and what your sexual orientation is based on a single photo of your face.[27] All of these projects are based on the assumption that algorithms can be created that will always be right, that won't have human biases, and that will function flawlessly, all the time. But decades of research has shown that this is almost never the case.

For the past decade, Google has attempted to predict what your search will be by suggesting possible search terms, a feature called auto-suggest or autocomplete, that is now fairly standard in almost any search

21 Beer, "The Social Power of Algorithms," 2.

22 Julia Powles, "New York City's Bold, Flawed Attempt to Make Algorithms Accountable," *The New Yorker,* December 20, 2017, https://www.newyorker.com/tech/annals-of-technology/new-york-citys-bold-flawed-attempt-to-make-algorithms-accountable.

23 O'Neil, "United Airlines Exposes Our Twisted Idea of Dignity."

24 Dwyer, "A Push to Expose the Computing Process in City Decision-Making."

25 Matthew Hutson, "Artificial Intelligence Could Identify Gang Crimes—and Ignite an Ethical Firestorm," *Science,* February 28, 2018, https://www.sciencemag.org/news/2018/02/artificial-intelligence-could-identify-gang-crimes-and-ignite-ethical-firestorm.

26 Sophia Chen, "AI Research Is in Desperate Need of an Ethical Watchdog," *WIRED,* September 18, 2017, https://www.wired.com/story/ai-research-is-in-desperate-need-of-an-ethical-watchdog/.

27 Sam Meredith, "A.I. Can Detect the Sexual Orientation of a Person Based on One Photo, Research Shows," *CNBC,* September 8, 2017, https://www.cnbc.com/2017/09/08/a-i-can-detect-the-sexual-orientation-of-a-person-based-on-one-photo-research-shows.html.

system. Professors at Lancaster University Paul Baker and Amanda Potts showed how the autosuggest function perpetuated stereotypes and biases around "identity terms," like "blacks," "muslims," "gays," and "women," finding that, among other things, "Gay people were negatively constructed as contracting AIDS, going to hell, not deserving equal rights, having high voices or talking like girls."[28] In 2016, Cadwalladr wrote about typing a search into Google, beginning with "are jews." Google's first autosuggest result for her was "are Jews evil?" Cadwalladr admits that "it's not a question I've ever thought of asking."[29] She clicked on the suggested search and looked at the "answers" Google provided: "nine out of ten which 'confirm'" that, indeed, Jews are evil.[30] First, Google's suggestion of "Are Jews evil?" was itself a fairly biased suggestion. And by returning primarily results from antisemitic websites, it perpetuates the bias. And it does so under the cloak of objectivity. (Cadwalladr also found that Google would suggest "are women evil?", and every one of the first ten results agreed that they are.)[31] This goes beyond merely incorrect search results and into the realm of bias. Jews and women are already marginalized, and to find that these stereotypes and prejudices are perpetuated by "objective" information tools is unsettling. When Cadwalladr asked Google about the results, they sent a response that absolved them of any responsibility:

> Our search results are a reflection of the content across the web. This means that sometimes unpleasant portrayals of sensitive subject matter online can affect what search results appear for a given query. These results don't reflect Google's own opinions or beliefs—as a company, we strongly value a diversity of perspectives, ideas and cultures.[32]

---

28 Paul Baker and Amanda Potts, "'Why Do White People Have Thin Lips?' Google and the Perpetuation of Stereotypes via Auto-Complete Search Forms," *Critical discourse studies* 10, no. 2 (2013): 197.

29 Cadwalladr, "Google, Democracy and the Truth About Internet Search."

30 Cadwalladr.

31 Cadwalladr.

32 Cadwalladr.

This wasn't the first time Google had run into trouble with antisemitic search results. In 2006, the antisemitic website jewwatch.org was the first result for a search of the word "jew." Google took the same approach, saying that the automated process might return offensive results, but there wasn't much they could do.[33] And more recently, biased autosuggest results have implied that the Ferguson riots were a hoax, that Michael Brown, the unarmed black man that was shot by police in Ferguson was a "thug," that the Parkland High School students who survived a mass shooting were "crisis actors," that "nazis are the new normal," and that climate change is a hoax.[34]

These results, often reflecting far right-wing viewpoints, exhibit bias because they appear in a public information retrieval tool. Bias often appears, according to Engin Bozdag, "when the system is used by a population with different values than those assumed in a design."[35] Bozdag was referring to bias against the user populations, but in this case, Google made an assumption that their algorithms could only be used to spread accurate, useful information rather than hate speech. Google is not alone. Recently, Facebook's COO Sheryl Sandberg admitted that the company had never considered whether someone would use their tools to discriminate against others: "We never intended or anticipated this functionality being used this way," she said.[36]

In the past few years, the study of bias in algorithms has exploded, as we have begun to come to grips with the enormous power we have ceded to algorithmically-driven systems. As I write this, Facebook is still reeling after a year of scrutiny over their role in spreading false and inflammatory information that may have affected the 2016 Presidential election. Google and other tech companies have been accused of biased search results

---

33   Cadwalladr.

34   Albright, ""#NotOKGoogle Search Suggestions."; Olivia Solon and Sam Levin, "How Google's Search Algorithm Spreads False Information With a Rightwing Bias," *The Guardian,* December 16, 2016, https://www.theguardian.com/technology/2016/dec/16/google-autocomplete-rightwing-bias-algorithm-political-propaganda.

35   Bozdag, "Bias in Algorithmic Filtering and Personalization," 222.

36   AJ Vicens, "Top Facebook Exec Sheryl Sandberg Just Apologized for Racist Ad Targeting," *Mother Jones,* September 20, 2017, https://www.motherjones.com/politics/2017/09/top-facebook-exec-sheryl-sandberg-just-apologized-for-racist-ad-targeting/.

against conservative voices. Academics and writers have also been publishing books on the subject over the past few years, some scholarly and some for the popular press.[37]

Simple assumptions baked into an algorithm can have significant effects. When the IBM team was training the AI-fed computer Watson to compete at the game show Jeopardy, it was asked the question "who was the first woman astronaut?" Watson answered "Wonder Woman,"" because in the chronological list of all the data it had been fed, the first reference to a flying woman in space was Wonder Woman. (No one mentioned if Watson also thought that Superman was the first man in space.) The algorithm had been created in such a way that it *assumed everything it read was true.* Researchers hoped to "tweak" the algorithm "to separate fictional references from real-world accounts."[38] But in this era of fake news, where it can be increasingly difficult for educated humans to sift through what is true and false, how will algorithms do this unless the humans who create them program them with specific parameters? (Incidentally, both Microsoft and Facebook have announced that they are developing algorithms that can detect bias in algorithms.[39])

Several conditions come together in the creation and use of algorithms that contribute to biased results. The first, and most obvious, are the business goals of the company. We have already looked at how Google is primarily an advertising company rather than a neutral information provider. This leads it to promote results that are popular, even if they are not the most accurate or useful, as Cadwalladr found when she searched for information on whether the holocaust was a hoax.[40] But bias does not have to be

---

37 Pasquale, *The Black Box Society;* Wachter-Boettcher, *Technically Wrong*; Noble, *Algorithms of Oppression*; Greenfield, *Radical Technologies*; Broussard, *Artificial Unintelligence*; Fry, *Hello World,* among others.

38 Lohr, *Data-ism,* 111.

39 Kyle Wiggers, "Microsoft Is Developing a Tool to Help Engineers Catch Bias in Algorithms," *VentureBeat,* May 25, 2018, https://venturebeat.com/2018/05/25/microsoft-is-developing-a-tool-to-help-engineers-catch-bias-in-algorithms/; Dave Gershgorn, "Facebook Says It Has a Tool to Detect Bias in Its Artificial Intelligence," *Quartz,* May 3, 2018, https://qz.com/1268520/facebook-says-it-has-a-tool-to-detect-bias-in-its-artificial-intelligence/.

40 Cadwalladr, "How to Bump Holocaust Deniers off Google's Top Spot?"

about racism, sexism, or bias against LGBTQ users. Here, the more common form of bias is commercial bias, where a company's own algorithms give preferential treatment to its services.

Back in 2007, Marissa Mayer admitted that Google Finance explicitly promoted Google's services over competitors. "It seems only fair right, we do all the work for the search page and all these other things ... That has actually been our policy, since then."[41] Yet Google itself on other occasions has said that it doesn't give preferential treatment to its own services, most notably in its defense against anti-trust litigation brought by the European Union in 2015.[42] Yet, Edelman and Lockwood showed that search engine results overrepresent services provided by the parent company.

> Search engines can use biased results to expand into new sectors, to grant instant free traffic to their own new services, and to block competitors and would-be competitors. The incentive for bias is all the stronger because the lack of obvious benchmarks makes most bias would be difficult to uncover.[43]

They note that this form of bias may not be as obvious as indexical bias, where merely reading the terms can allow users to see the issues, but by manipulating the results for their own services, search engine companies "can affect where users go online" by promoting their own services high in their results.[44]

Amazon has also been accused of using its algorithm to give itself an edge over independent sellers that sell on the Amazon platform.[45] And in the library world, ProQuest/Ex Libris and EBSCO, two of the largest licensed content vendors are also two of the large library discovery vendors. They each claim that they don't prioritize their own content over their

---

41   Edelman and Lockwood, "Measuring Bias in"Organic" Web Search."

42   David Lumb, "Read Google's Defensive Response To European Antitrust Charges," *Fast Company,* April 16, 2015, https://www.fastcompany.com/3045132/read-googles-defensive-response-to-european-antitrust-charges.

43   Edelman and Lockwood, "Measuring Bias in 'Organic' Web Search."

44   Edelman and Lockwood.

45   Angwin and Mattu, "Amazon Says It Puts Customers First."

competitors, but these claims are difficult to reconcile with what we know about their actual business practices.[46] For instance, Ex Libris's discovery service Summon (and its 360 Link link resolver) use a technology called Index Enhanced Direct Linking, which bypasses a typical link resolver screen if the discovery service knows it has a reliable link directly to the content the user wants.[47] Since the most reliable links Summon's index has in its index are those that link to ProQuest's licensed content databases, it will naturally send people to ProQuest databases more often than EBSCO databases. And this is doubly true since EBSCO notoriously does not share all of its content metadata with other discovery services,[48] making the linking from a ProQuest/Ex Libris discovery service to an EBSCO article problematic.[49] Of course, because EBSCO has its own metadata in its index, and relies on what other services provide, its rich in-house metadata also suggests that users will be more likely to land on an EBSCO database than a ProQuest one.

But sometimes business goals result in more than just commercial bias in results. Over the past few years Facebook has weathered a number of crises surrounding its business practices: the rise of fake news and political propaganda on its News Feed, fake user accounts used to promote hate groups, advertising policies that allowed advertisers to bypass civil rights legislation and target specific racial or ethnic groups, or specifically target users based on racist and antisemitic "interests" like "jew haters," and more.

---

46   Galvan, "Architecture of Authority;" Simon Barron and Andrew Preater, "Critical systems librarianship," in *The Politics and the practice of critical librarianship*, eds. Karen P. Nicholson and Maura Seale (Sacramento, CA: Library Juice Press, 2018), 93.

47   "Summon: Index-Enhanced Direct Linking to Provider Content," Ex Libris Knowledge Center, February 21, 2014, https://knowledge.exlibrisgroup.com/Summon/Product_Documentation/Configuring_The_Summon_Service/Direct_Linking_in_the_Summon_Service/Summon%3A_Index-Enhanced_Direct_Linking_to_Provider_Content.

48   "EBSCO Open Collaboration Policy for Technical Interoperability and Bibliographic Record Sharing," *EBSCO,* June 2018, https://www.ebsco.com/open-collaboration-policy.

49   This is a common topic on the professional list-servs for library discovery customers. EBSCO's sharing policy reads like a passive-aggressive letter between bitter rivals, promising to share "basic bibliographic records" and full text for searching with "discovery services from partner companies that share EBSCO's desire to support customers through true collaboration." See EBSCO, "EBSCO Open Collaboration Policy for Technical Interoperability and Bibliographic Record Sharing."

Wachter-Boettcher writes that "Facebook may not have intended to surface traumatic content, just like it didn't intend to let advertisers post hateful or nefarious ads. But it *did* intend to prioritize rapid growth and user engagement over all else."[50] Their business model made these kinds of unanticipated results commonplace.

Aside from business goals, the worldview and assumptions of the people who make algorithmic tools also contribute to bias in algorithmic systems. Wachter-Boettcher wrote about how Facebook and Google both have a culture of believing you can "engineer your way out of anything."[51] *New York Times* columnist Fareed Manjoo, writing about Facebook's News Feed's role in the misinformation campaign during the 2016 US Presidential election, notes that Facebook sees the News Feed as "an engineering problem rather than an editorial one."[52] Mark Zuckerberg described the News Feed as a tool to help people decide whether or not their "experience today was meaningful," which he equated to a complex "math problem."[53] A software engineer is the only person I could think of that would think determining whether or not something was "meaningful" had anything to do with the kind of universality and precision that mathematics brings to bear. But this is precisely how algorithms work, by converting "items, actions and processes into calculable and malleable units or data points—rendering all (objects, actions and relations) in some senses as equivalent regardless of the actual content or context."[54] The team that works on the News Feed, writes Manjoo, is "concerned only with quantifiable outcomes about people's actions on the site. That data, at Facebook, is the only real truth."[55]

---

50   Sara Wachter-Boettcher, "Facebook Treats Its Ethical Failures Like Software Bugs, and That's Why They Keep Happening," *Quartz,* October 20, 2017, https://qz.com/1107036/facebook-treats-its-ethical-failures-like-software-bugs-and-thats-why-they-keep-happening/.

51   Wachter-Boettcher, *Technically Wrong,* 170.

52   Faheed Manjoo, "Can Facebook Fix Its Own Worst Bug?," *New York Times,* April 25, 2017, https://www.nytimes.com/2017/04/25/magazine/can-facebook-fix-its-own-worst-bug.html.

53   Manjoo.

54   Willson, "Algorithms (and the) Everyday," 147.

55   Manjoo, "Can Facebook Fix Its Own Worst Bug?"

This is a common refrain from software engineers. Manjoo quotes Joshua Reeves, co-founder of the human-resources startup Gusto as saying "I have this engineering brain that wants to go to this analytical, rational, nonemotional way of looking at things."[56] As we saw in Chapter 1, Lohr interviews several engineers who prefer to see the world through the lens of math. Shery Turkle, the Abby Rockefeller Mauzé Professor of the Social Studies of Science and Technology at the Massachusetts Institute of Technology, said about the late computer scientist, writer, and refugee from Nazi Germany Joseph Weizenbaum, that he "held deep convictions about the kinds of intellectual values that might prevent people from trivializing human life. He saw these as decidedly absent from the engineering-style of thinking ... that characterized computer culture."[57] The way that software engineers are taught to solve problems, by assuming that everything can be expressed as an equation, leads to this dehumanization of the subjects of the tools. Even MacCormick, an engineer writing about the impact of algorithms, feels compelled to remind readers that "no matter how many clever algorithms are invented in the future, there will always be problems whose answers are 'uncomputable'."[58] Not everything is countable, and it is very hard to find humanity in a column of numbers. Eventually, even areas that are difficult to quantify will need to be manipulated to work with algorithms. As Turkle noted over 20 years ago before the age of algorithms, "if the computer needs rules in order to work, then areas of knowledge in which rules had previously been unimportant must formulate them or perish."[59]

Many software engineers hold that algorithms are a better tool for making decisions, because they are more understandable than human decision making. This is a claim put forth in an op-ed in the *New York Times* by the venture capitalist and former academic Vijay Pande, when he wrote that "compared with human intelligence, A.I. [artificial intelligence] is

56 Manjoo.

57 Sherry Turkle, *Life on the Screen: Identity in the Age of the Internet* (New York: Simon and Schuster, 1997), 106.

58 MacCormick, *9 Algorithms That Changed the Future,* 174.

59 Turkle, *Life on the Screen,* 107.

actually the more transparent of intelligences."[60] The presumption here is that machine learning algorithms (which is another term for artificial intelligence) can be made intelligible whereas we do not have access to how other humans are thinking through things and understanding the world. In effect, the engineers are using the argument of an unknowable black box and pointing it at the human mind, rather than these complex nests of computer code. Yet much of this view rests on the assumption that the human mind functions like a computer. Entrepreneur Ambarish Mitra, writing in *Quartz,* argued that we can train algorithms to be "moral" by "collect[ing] data on what each and every person thinks is the right thing to do. … With enough inputs, we could utilize AI to analyze these massive data sets…and drive ourselves toward a better system of morality."[61] This is all possible because he begins with an explicit assumption: "because morality is a derivation of humanity, a perfect moral system exists somewhere in our consciousness." All we have to do, he says "should simply be a matter of collection and analyzing massive amounts of data on human opinions and conditions and producing the correct result."[62] That sounds like the opposite of "simple."

But this critique also ignores the fact that all of us have access to our own minds, and that we have managed to communicate with one another for millennia. Eubanks writes that she finds

> the philosophy that sees human beings as unknowable black boxes and machines as transparent deeply troubling. It seems to be a worldview that surrenders any attempt at empathy and forecloses the possibility of ethical developments. The presumption that human decision-making is opaque and inaccessible is an admission that we have abandoned a social commitment to try to understand each other.[63]

---

60 Vijay Pande, "Artificial Intelligence's 'Black Box' Is Nothing to Fear," *New York Times,* January 25, 2018, https://www.nytimes.com/2018/01/25/opinion/artificial-intelligence-black-box.html.

61 Ambarish Mitra, "We Can Train AI to Identify Good and Evil, and Then Use It to Teach Us Morality," *Quartz,* April 5, 2018, https://qz.com/1244055/we-can-train-ai-to-identify-good-and-evil-and-then-use-it-to-teach-us-morality/.

62 Mitra.

63 Eubanks, *Automating Inequality,* 168.

One reason for this mindset is the emphasis on technical skills in college and university engineering programs. Noble notes that most engineers, "through no fault of their own, are underexposed to the critical thinking and learning about history and culture afforded by the social sciences and humanities in most colleges of engineering nationwide."[64] In part because of this lack of training, we are seeing more and more biased outcomes from our algorithmic systems.

Lohr shares a story about a team of talented engineers that Jeffrey Hammerbacher hired to write the algorithms that sift through big data sets to improve health care. He begins his report on their working style by noting that "seven young men sit at a round table,"[65] "all in their late twenties to early thirties."[66] Where are the women? Those with more life and work experience? We don't learn the ethnicities or racial backgrounds of the engineers, but based on industry numbers, we can assume that most were white. As Broussard noted, "computer systems are proxies for the people who made them."[67] Because algorithmic systems are created by people, the personal beliefs, values, and experiences of those people will necessarily find their way into any product they create.

The Swedish journalist Andreas Ekström, in his *TED* talk on algorithmic bias, reminded us that "no code can ever completely eradicate"[68] those values. And our values and beliefs are informed by who we are, meaning that small teams of mostly white men in their late 20s and early 30s are going to bake their personal beliefs into the software that we all interact with every day. In 2016, *The Atlantic's* annual "Pulse of the Technology Industry" survey showed that men were far more likely to see the technology industry as a meritocracy than women.[69] And Broussard notes that because the world is unequal, when we build our tools from the viewpoint of white men, then those who are already discriminated against—"women

---

64   Noble, *Algorithms of Oppression*, 163.

65   Lohr, *Data-ism*, 177.

66   Lohr, 180.

67   Broussard, *Artificial Unintelligence*, 67.

68   Andreas Ekström, "The Moral Bias Behind Your Search Results," *TED,* January 2015, https://www.ted.com/talks/andreas_ekstrom_the_moral_bias_behind_your_search_results.

69   Wachter-Boettcher, *Technically Wrong*, 175.

and minority people"—will continue to experience bias and inequality in the digital realm. She quips, "Math people are often surprised by this; women and poor and minority people are not surprised by this."[70]

Often the default assumptions of white men lead them to overlook methodological flaws in their tools that lead to biased outcomes.[71] Eubanks highlights how engineers created automation tools for the State of Indiana's welfare recipients that

> were based on time-worn, race- and class-motivated assumptions about welfare recipients that were encoded into performance metrics and programmed into business processes: they are lazy and must be "prodded" into contributing to their own support, they are sneaky and prone to fraudulent claims, and their burdensome use of public resources must be repeatedly discouraged.[72]

This isn't limited to stereotypes of the poor. The computer science researcher Paul Viola created a software program that would detect objects in images. While it was able to identify faces, it had trouble with Asian and black faces in particular. Journalist Elizabeth Dwoskin wrote about how Viola "eventually traced the error back to the source: In his original data set of about 5,000 images, whites predominated."[73] A 2011 study by the National Institute of Standards and Technology (NIST) that showed that when facial recognition software is created by Asian developers in Asian countries, it is more reliable at recognizing Asian faces.[74] Joy Buolamani, a black woman who studies facial recognition software at the MIT Media Lab, at times wears a white mask so that the software will recognize her face, since it performs much better with white faces than with Asian or black faces. Pointing to the lack

---

70 Broussard, *Artificial Unintelligence,* 115.

71 Wakabayashi, "Trump Says Google Is Rigged, Despite Its Denials."

72 Eubanks, *Automating Inequality,* 81.

73 Elizabeth Dwoskin, "How Social Bias Creeps Into Web Technology; Software Can Lead to Unintended Errors, Potentially Unfair Outcomes," *Wall Street Journal,* August 21, 2015, https://www.wsj.com/articles/computers-are-showing-their-biases-and-tech-firms-are-concerned-1440102894.

74 Ali Breland, "White code, black faces," *Logic,* 3 (2018): 199.

of diversity in the field, she emphasizes that "who codes matters."[75] But, as Wachter-Boettcher laments, the tech industry "wants diversity *numbers*, but doesn't want to disrupt its culture to get or keep diverse *people*."[76]

Engineers often are the most important and most rewarded of the employees of technology companies. So we have an industry that is mostly populated with white men, and those employees are paid more and given more power than roles that tend to have more women in them, such as communications-related jobs.[77] The viewpoints of this mostly homogeneous group of people then get baked into the products that make choices for us every day. And because of the veneer of objectivity these tools are marketed with, engineers are not always asked to take responsibility for their work. In early 2018, an engineer who helped create the algorithm to determine whether a crime was gang related was asked what would happen if someone was mistakenly labeled a gang member because of the algorithm? What steps the engineers had taken to make sure the training data wasn't biased? And whether they were also developing algorithms to help heavily-policed neighborhoods predict when police were going to raid? The Harvard engineer, Hau Chan, didn't have answers for any of these concerns. "I'm just an engineer," he said.[78] The audience member who questioned him quoted a song before walking out: "Once the rockets are up, who cares where they come down?"[79] At the same time we are treating engineers as the most valuable contributors to our society, we are not asking them to be responsible for their work and actions.

When we look at an example of an engineer like former Google employee James Damore, who published a memo at Google arguing that women were biologically unqualified to be engineers, we have to wonder how that viewpoint affects the products he was working on. Broussard notes that the technology industry will "pardon a whole host of antisocial behaviors

---

75   Joy Buolamwini, "How I'm Fighting Bias in Algorithms," *TED,* November 2016, https://www.ted.com/talks/joy_buolamwini_how_i_m_fighting_bias_in_algorithms.

76   Wachter-Boettcher, *Technically Wrong,* 184.

77   Wachter-Boettcher, 21.

78   Hutson, "Artificial intelligence could identify gang crimes—and ignite an ethical firestorm."

79   Hutson.

because the perpetrators are geniuses."[80] The tech industry's perspective is that "efficient code is prioritized above human interactions."[81] Noble calls out the conflict between Google's public stance as a company (apologizing for antisemitic results by saying that they really do value diversity) and the personal values openly espoused by engineers like Damore that make these supposedly neutral products. How can these employees both promote sexist and racist views and also claim to be building objective tools, she asks?[82] Willson notes that when engineers create algorithms to act upon data in the world, that data is likely not being analyzed "in terms of its political or social values explicitly."[83]

Important aspects of our lived-experience are being ignored in the rush to quantify every aspect of our lives. Principal Researcher at Microsoft Research and the founder and president of the Data & Society Research Institute danah boyd emphasizes that without this kind of explicit training to build empathy and ethical awareness, we're going to keep having problems, for without "clear direction, they're [engineers] going to build something that affects peoples' lives in unexpected ways."[84] What's more, without carefully looking at the values and expectations of the people who the tool is for, Noble reminds us it will lead to more biased tools "that come at the expense of people of color and women."[85] Researching users is always important, as designer Erica Hall notes, since a nearly homogeneous group of young men designing for themselves will lead to "building discrimination right into your product."[86] Broussard reminds us that "being good with computers is not the same as being good with people."[87] She and Noble both call for the need for engineering teams to understand how social and cultural systems work within history.

---

80   Broussard, *Artificial Unintelligence,* 75.

81   Broussard, 75.

82   Noble, *Algorithms of Oppression,* 2.

83   Willson, "Algorithms (and the) Everyday," 145.

84   Dwyer, "A Push to Expose the Computing Process in City Decision-Making."

85   Noble, *Algorithms of Oppression,* 70.

86   Erica Hall, *Just Enough Research* (New York: A Book Apart, 2013), 79.

87   Broussard, *Artificial Unintelligence,* 83.

Several thinkers have noted the correlation between a push in society to elevate automated tools created by white men and the civil rights gains for women and minorities. O'Neil notes that the poor are affected by automated systems far more than the middle-class or wealthy classes.[88] Broussard looks back at the Industrial Revolution and sees a choice made by the ruling class to feed the ever-expanding need for workers. "One option was to enact social change (emancipation, universal suffrage, breaking down class barriers) and develop the existing workforce by allowing all people who weren't elite white men greater access to education and train these workers for jobs."[89] Instead, they chose to create machines to do the work. In the late twentieth century, Noble notes, it was not a coincidence that the civil rights gains and the feminist revolution of the sixties that gave women and minorities more access to make the choices that affected their lives happened at the same time the largely white engineering class began talking about how much better machines were at making decisions than people.[90] And Eubanks often reminds engineers to do a "gut-check" when creating an algorithmic tool by asking whether the non-poor would accept the system being used on them.[91]

It is important to note, as Seaver reminds us, that not every engineer thinks about algorithmic systems in the same way.[92] In the past few years in particular, employees have been standing up to what they see as bias in algorithmic systems. At many companies, "engineers and technologists are increasingly asking whether the products they are working on are being used for surveillance ... or military projects."[93] Interns at Redfin, a real-estate startup, grilled the CEO about whether the design of the

---

88   O'Neil, *Weapons of Math Destruction,* 8.

89   Broussard, *Artificial Unintelligence,* 78.

90   Noble, *Algorithms of Oppression,* 168–69.

91   Eubanks, *Automating Inequality,* 211–12.

92   Michael Todd, "Nick Seaver on Dissecting the Algorithmic Organism," *Method Space,* February 15, 2018, https://www.methodspace.com/nick-seaver-dissecting-algorithmic-organism/.

93   Kate Conger and Cade Metz, "Tech Workers Now Want to Know: What Are We Building This For?," *New York Times,* October 7, 2018, https://www.nytimes.com/2018/10/07/technology/tech-workers-ask-censorship-surveillance.html.

site encouraged socio-economic divides because of the way the design emphasized school information and test scores.[94] In early November of 2018, thousands of Google employees walked out for hours in protest for the way the company's leadership handled sexual harassment and abuse cases.[95] So there appears to be a growing awareness in the industry to these issues. But Gillespie emphasizes that these issues stem from much more than whether bias is encoded into the decision points of each algorithm. Rather "it's the institutionalization of procedure over human judgment, the metrification of complex phenomena, and the opacity of the values it depends on."[96]

Another factor that contributes to the increasingly biased outputs of algorithms are a dependence on proxies to measure factors that the tool's creators think are important. Wachter-Boettcher defines a proxy as "a stand-in for real knowledge."[97] Often, the information needed by the creators of an algorithm isn't available or easily quantified. Greenfield uses the examples of "average walking speed stands in for the more inchoate 'pace' of urban life, while the number of patent applications constitute an index of innovation."[98] But once we replace actual people with quantifiable proxy data, we run the risk of dehumanizing the users of a tool. "It's not easy to remember that each row in a dataset represents a real person with hopes, dreams, a family, and a history," Broussard reminds us.[99]

Facebook, like most companies, measures easily-quantifiable things like Daily Average Users (DAUs) and Monthly Average Users (MAU). But they also use a metric called "CAUs," or Cares About Us.[100] How do they measure whether a user cares about Facebook? Through proxies, like how likely they are to come back to Facebook even if they have problems with

---

94 Conger and Metz.

95 Kate Conger and Daisuke Wakabayashi, "Google Overhauls Sexual Misconduct Policy After Employee Walkout," *New York Times,* November 8, 2018, https://www.nytimes.com/2018/11/08/technology/google-arbitration-sexual-harassment.html/

96 Tarleton Gillespie, Twitter Post, March 21, 2018, 6:53am, https://twitter.com/TarletonG/status/976456851025006592.

97 Wachter-Boettcher, *Technically Wrong,* 110.

98 Greenfield, *Radical Technologies,* 56–57.

99 Broussard, *Artificial Unintelligence,* 109.

100 Wachter-Boettcher, *Technically Wrong,* 97.

the site. In one study, Facebook intentionally made its Android app crash repeatedly, just so they could measure how likely a user would be to come back after the crash.[101] But this doesn't actually measure how much a user cares about Facebook: most users are not going to Facebook for Facebook, they are going to connect with friends, coworkers, community, or read news and other content. How often users visit even in the face of technical problems is not a direct measurement of "care," it's a proxy (and not a very good one, at that).

The problem with using proxies in a system that claims to be objective and neutral is that "proxies are bound to be inexact and often unfair."[102] Zip codes are often used as proxy data, despite zip codes also being a proxy for economic class and race. Credit scores are a very common proxy for all sorts of things that have little to do with extending credit, from how likely you are to be a good tenant to whether you will be a good employee. But as O'Neil notes, "a sterling credit rating is not just a proxy for responsibility and smart decisions. It is also a proxy for wealth. And wealth is highly correlated with race."[103] Popularity is another common proxy, standing in for concepts like "good" or "useful" or "true." Many autosuggest algorithms simply collect popular queries to show to future searchers, assuming that popularity is a proxy for a good or useful search. (And users see those suggested searches and questions as boundaries around truth.) In one study, researchers created an algorithm that decided whether a selfie was "good" or not, by using whether an selfie image was popular as a proxy for "good." As Broussard notes, "by selecting for popularity, the data scientists created a model that had significant bias: it prioritized young, white, cisgendered images of women that fit a narrow, heteonormative definition of attractiveness."[104] To paraphrase Inigo Montoya from *The Princess Bride*, "That proxy, it does not measure what you think it measures."

---

101   Christina Farr, "Report: Facebook Tested User Loyalty By Sabotaging Its Android App," *Fast Company*, January 4, 2016, https://www.fastcompany.com/3055089/report-facebook-tested-user-loyalty-by-sabotaging-its-android-app.

102   O'Neil, *Weapons of Math Destruction*, 108.

103   O'Neil, 149.

104   Broussard, *Artificial Unintelligence*, 150.

Because proxy data isn't measuring what algorithmic creators claim to be measuring, "proxy data can actually make a system *less* accurate over time."[105] In addition, as Eubanks notes, using proxies while claiming objectivity and neutrality is disingenuous: "the choice of proxy variables, even the choice to use proxies at all, reflects human discretion."[106] But proxies are more convenient, as O'Neil notes, "because proxies are easier to manipulate than the complicated reality they represent."[107]

At times, it isn't proxy data that introduces bias, but rather the data itself. When Eubanks researched the algorithms in use by Pennsylvania's Allegheny County that use data from public sources of support to predict child abuse and other family problems, middle class and wealthier families were less likely to raise flags because they had no previous data in the system. Middle class and wealthier familes did not use public sources of support, but rather used "nannies, babysitters, private therapists, Alcoholics Anonymous, and luxury rehabilitation centers,"[108] which do not provide data to the county system. The professional class would not allow their private data to be used, but the assumption is that data from poor families is fair game. Distinguished Research Professor at NYU and a Principal Researcher at Microsoft Research New York, Kate Crawford, noted that Amazon's same-day delivery service, which works only in certain zip codes, was not available for predominantly black neighborhoods. "The areas overlooked were remarkable similar to those affected by mortgage redlining in the mid-20th century."[109]

Perhaps one of the biggest issues with bias in algorithmic systems is in the machine learning libraries that underlie many of the algorithmic systems in use today. Many algorithmic systems that need to understand language use a data set called the Common Crawl, which contains some 840 billion words.[110] Another common language data set is Word2Vec. Both

---

105 Wachter-Boettcher, *Technically Wrong,* 111.

106 Eubanks, *Automating Inequality,* 167.

107 O'Neil, *Weapons of Math Destruction,* 55.

108 Eubanks, *Automating Inequality,* 157.

109 Crawford, "Artificial Intelligence's White Guy Problem."

110 Annalee Newitz, "Princeton Researchers Discover Why AI Become Racist and Sexist," *Ars Technica,* April 18, 2017, https://arstechnica.com/science/2017/04/princeton-scholars-figure-out-why-your-ai-is-racist/.

tools were created by scanning digital examples of language, mostly from the Internet. The assumption is that Word2Vec and the Common Crawl will be able to look across their large data sets and find the "relationships between words as mathematical values," which "makes it possible for a machine to perceive semantic connections between, say, 'king' and 'queen' and understand that the relationship between the two words is similar to that between 'man' and 'woman.'"[111]

One problem is that the Internet is full of hate speech and bias, but even more troublesome is that systemic gender and racial biases are embedded in the language used every day online, even if not in explicitly biased ways. But the machine learning algorithms picked that up from the data. Researchers found that the tools saw the word "programmer" as being related to the word "man," and that "the most similar word for 'woman' is 'homemaker'."[112]

And bias in data sets isn't limited to word parsing, either. Remember Paul Viola, the researcher who found that his training data used predominately white faces? Google and Flickr have had similar issues, when their algorithms for identifying items in photos labeled black people as gorillas or apes.[113] Nikon's cameras misread Asian faces as blinking, and Hewlett-Packard's web cameras couldn't see darked-skinned users.[114] Joy Buolamwini notes that facial recognition libraries, written mostly by white engineers, are built on preexisting code libraries that have also been written by white engineers, meaning that they often don't recognize non-white faces

---

111 Will Knight, "How to Fix Silicon Valley's Sexist Algorithms," *MIT Technology Review,* November 23, 2016, https://www.technologyreview.com/s/602950/how-to-fix-silicon-valleys-sexist-algorithms/.

112 Tolga Bolukbasi et al., "Man Is to Computer Programmer as Woman Is to Homemaker? Debiased Word Embeddings," (2016), https://arxiv.org/abs/1607.06520; Knight, "How to Fix Silicon Valley's Sexist Algorithms;" Wiggers, "Microsoft Is Developing a Tool to Help Engineers Catch Bias in Algorithms."

113 Jana Kasperkevic, "Google Says Sorry for Racist Auto-Tag in Photo App," *The Guardian,* July 1, 2015, https://www.theguardian.com/technology/2015/jul/01/google-sorry-racist-auto-tag-photo-app; Alex Hern, "Flickr Faces Complaints Over 'Offensive' Auto-Tagging for Photos," *The Guardian,* May 20, 2015, https://www.theguardian.com/technology/2015/may/20/flickr-complaints-offensive-auto-tagging-photos.

114 Crawford, "Artificial Intelligence's White Guy Problem."

very well.[115] And Simonite reports that two of the most commonly used research image collections "display a predictable gender bias in their depiction of activities such as cooking and sports. Images of shopping and washing are linked to women, for example, while coaching and shooting are tied to men."[116] Narayanan also notes that many of these correlations are culture specific, so we're also baking in Western ideas of what certain things "look like." On Twitter, he noted that "any attempt to 'accurately' label images as bride/bridegroom simply codifies stereotypes about what brides/bridegrooms are supposed to look like."[117] The problem extends beyond identification in words and images, and into these companies' business practices. Google's personalization tools have been shown to display ads for high paying jobs six times more often to men than women.[118] More recently, Anja Lambrechy of the London Business School and Catherine E. Tucker of MIT showed how fewer women see ads for STEM jobs, even when the algorithm was designed to be gender-neutral.[119] These machine learning data sets are matching genders with other keywords that they deem related based on their training data, which is often full of assumptions and systemic bias.

This hits on the real danger with tools like Word2Vec, which are being used to build all the other tools that rely on understanding language, like recommendation engines and search engines, "all without considering the implications of relying on data that reflects the historical biases and outdated norms to make future predictions."[120] FaceApp, a photography app, created a "hotness" filter that used machine-learning techniques to determine what made a person "beautiful." The filter lightened skin tones and

---

115 Breland, "White Code, Black Faces," 198.

116 Tom Simonite, "Machines Taught by Photos Learn a Sexist View of Women," *WIRED*, August 21, 2017, https://www.wired.com/story/machines-taught-by-photos-learn-a-sexist-view-of-women/.

117 Arvind Narayanan, Twitter Post, March 20, 2018, 8:25am, https://twitter.com/random_walker/status/976117562500055040.

118 Dwoskin, "How Social Bias Creeps Into Web Technology."

119 Anja Lambrecht and Catherine E. Tucker, "Algorithmic Bias? An Empirical Study Into Apparent Gender-Based Discrimination in the Display of STEM Career Ads," March 9, 2018, http://dx.doi.org/10.2139/ssrn.2852260.

120 Wachter-Boettcher, *Technically Wrong*, 139.

made people look more "white." Writing about the user outrage, journalist Natasha Lomas noted that "frankly it would be hard to come up with a better (visual) example of the risks of bias being embedded within algorithms."[121] Companies like HireVue, the human resources company that makes software for automating applicant interviews I described in Chapter 1, "compares a candidate's word choice, tone, and facial movements with the body language and vocabularies of their [the company's] best hires."[122] The result is an algorithm that continues to discriminate against those who are different from your existing workforce, ensuring little to no diversity in new hires. By encasing the bias in the supposed objectivity of data and algorithms, the company avoids answering to the bias it enforces in the hiring process. In 2014, the White House released a report on the dangers of prioritizing data over people. "Big data analytics have the potential to eclipse longstanding civil rights protections in how personal information is used by housing, credit, employment, health, education, and the marketplace,"[123] they wrote.

It is important to remember that problem results, including bias, are primarily "a result of the algorithmic outcomes and interactions with other social systems and practices—as a result of their [algorithms] engagement with people."[124] As Seaver noted, we must understand algorithms as systems, and not isolated bits of code.[125] Noble reminds us that now, more than ever in this time of racial and political tension, we must be mindful of the implications of seemingly objective systems presenting information to users who are looking for answers about race and race relations. Often, as we have seen, these people are being led to fascist websites, antisemitic websites, and white supremacist websites.

---

121 Natasha Lomas, "FaceApp Apologizes for Building a Racist AI," *TechCrunch*, April 25, 2017, https://techcrunch.com/2017/04/25/faceapp-apologises-for-building-a-racist-ai/.

122 Torres, "New App Scans Your Face and Tells Companies Whether You're Worth Hiring."

123 Executive Office of the President, *Big Data: Seizing Opportunities, Preserving Values*, May 1, 2014, https://obamawhitehouse.archives.gov/sites/default/files/docs/big_data_privacy_report_may_1_2014.pdf.

124 Willson, "Algorithms (and the) everyday," 144.

125 Seaver, "Knowing algorithms."

> The power of search engines to lead people to a breadth and depth of information cannot be more powerfully illustrated than by looking at Dylann Roof's own alleged words about using Google to find information about the Trayvon Martin murder, which led to his racial identity development."[126]

That development, of course, led to the murder of nine innocent people.

These are not the only pathways for bias to enter algorithms, but they are the most relevant. They also undermine the claim that these algorithmic systems are objective and neutral. And as we begin to look more closely at library discovery systems, we will see the same kinds of misguided thinking behind wrong and biased results in our libraries' tools.

---

126   Noble, *Algorithms of Oppression*, 115.

Chapter 5 Bias in Library Discovery

Bias in library discovery systems is merely the latest example of bias in LIS practices. Researchers over the past 50 years have investigated the racial, gender, and sexual orientation bias in library classification systems, showing how "theoretically neutral library activities like cataloging have often recreated societal patterns of exclusion and inequality."[1] In her 2002 investigation of gender discrimination in the Library of Congress Subject Headings (LCSH) and the Dewey Decimal System, Librarian Hope Olson argues that "the library catalogue is not a neutral tool. [Rather,] it is constructed. Hence, it does not just passively reflect the dominant values of society in some neutral or objective manner, but selects those values for expression."[2] As Noble notes, these selections "rely on human decisions" where "social context and histories or exploitation or objectification are not taken into explicit consideration—rather, they are disavowed."[3]

Olson notes that "until 1996, 'Man' was still used as a generic term for humanity in LCSH, representing the dominant member of a hierarchy, standing as the universal or norm."[4] As Librarian Joan Marshall wrote

---

1 Bess Sadler and Chris Bourg, "Feminism and the Future of Library Discovery," *Code4ib Journal* 28 (2015), https://journal.code4lib.org/articles/10425.

2 Hope A. Olson, *The Power to Name: Locating the Limits of Subject Representation in Libraries* (Dordrecht, Netherlands: Kluwer Academic Publishers, 2002), 2.

3 Noble, *Algorithms of Oppression,* 144.

4 Olson, *The Power to Name,* 149.

30 years before Olson, "the 'majority reader' and the norm, as far as LC [Library of Congress] is concerned, is white, Christian (often specifically Protestant), male, and straight."[5] Olson notes that some subjects make it clear that the male gender is universal, by adding "Women" to a category to differentiate, such as "Women Writers." There is no complementary "Men Writers" subject, so "Writers" is assumed to be made up of men. In other cases such as the subject heading "Prostitutes," there is a separate category for "Male prostitutes," but not a specific one for women, indicating that prostitutes are women, and men are the exception.[6] Librarian and writer Barbara Fister notes that this gender bias still exists today, since LCSH "treats women as a category subordinate to families."[7]

These issues continue to cause conflict. In 2016, Melissa Padilla, an immigrant from Mexico and a senior at Dartmouth, noted that LCSH labeled all undocumented immigrants as "illegal aliens."[8] Noble notes that these kinds of classifications are part of a long tradition of "naming members of society as problem people," such as LC's former subject heading the "Jewish question," which wasn't changed to "Jews" until 1984, or the labeling of Asian Americans' with the subject heading "Yellow peril."[9] It was no surprise when the push by Padilla and others to update the subject "illegal aliens" was met with fierce resistance by right-wing politicians.[10] Noble reminds us that "control over identity is political and often a matter of public policy."[11]

These issues are also operating in the background of library discovery systems, since many of these tools harness problematic metadata in opaque ways to return results.

---

5   Joan K. Marshall, "LC Labeling: An indictment," in *Revolting Librarians*, eds. Celeste West and Elizabeth Katz (San Francisco: Booklegger Press, 1972), 46.

6   Olson, *The Power to Name*, 156.

7   Barbara Fister, "The Bigot in the Machine," *Inside Higher Ed:Babelfish* (blog), March 17, 2016, https://www.insidehighered.com/blogs/library-babel-fish/bigot-machine.

8   The Editorial Board, "A Fight Over 'Aliens'," *New York Times*, June 20, 2016, https://www.nytimes.com/2016/06/20/opinion/a-fight-over-aliens.html.

9   Noble, *Algorithms of Oppression*, 135.

10   The Editorial Board, "A Fight Over 'Aliens'."

11   Noble, *Algorithms of Oppression*, 135.

For this research, I investigated four library discovery systems, with varying degrees of access to each: Ex Libris' Summon and Primo, OCLC's WorldCat Discovery, and EBSCO's EDS. Since library discovery systems are licensed by individual libraries, there was no way to conduct a controlled study with the same holdings in the index across all platforms. And little research has been done comparing the different systems (unless you count the little digs and jabs alluded to in marketing brochures). In the years after WorldCat Local (a precursor to WorldCat Discovery) and Summon became the first commercially-available library discovery services, a handful of libraries have published usability tests comparing one or more of the systems, often during a trial period while the institution weighs its options to determine which system to license. One of the earliest studies by Andrew Asher, Lynda M. Duke, and Suzanne Wilson reported that EDS, Summon, Google Scholar, and library databases "perform similarly but function differently."[12] Furthermore,

> By structuring and ordering the way information is seen and found, any search interface exerts a form of epistemological power by virtue of their relevancy ranking algorithms. The judgments embedded within these systems are often opaque and unclear for the user, but unfortunately they appear to be internalized by many, if not most, students, who routinely trust whatever results a search engine returns.[13]

Because these systems bear a remarkable resemblance to one another, it is easy for users to assume that they will all give the same results for similar searches. But in fact, the combination of different centralized indexes, varied collection development practices at subscribing institutions, and competing relevancy algorithms means that it is unlikely that these systems will return the same results for the same searches. Even within similar searches, discovery services can return very different results. For instance, in Summon, a search for "the bible" returns a Topic Explorer entry for the Wikipedia article "The Bible and Homosexuality" (shown in Figure 5.1), while just

---

12   Asher, Duke, and Wilson, "Paths of discovery," 477.

13   Asher, Duke, and Wilson, 477.

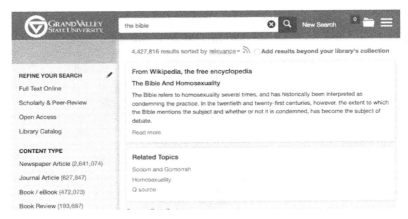

Figure 5.1   Summon search for "the bible" showing Wikipedia entry.

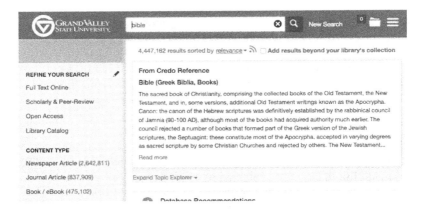

Figure 5.2   Summon search for "bible" showing Credo entry.

searching for "bible" (or "holy bible," for that matter) will return an entry on "Bible" from Credo, which actually explains the historical significance of the book (Figure 5.2).

Because Summon's algorithms for the Topic Explorer are black boxed, we don't know why adding a stop word like "the" (which many search systems will simply ignore) causes such different responses in the results.

A year after Asher, Lane, and Wilson's study, Karen Ciccone and John Vickery ran a similar study comparing Summon, EDS, and Google Scholar for North Carolina State University Libraries. Here, the number of "relevant" results was considered, with relevant being defined as "if it [the result] matched the presumed topic of the user's search."[14] In previous chapters, we have already discussed the problems with that approach, but nonetheless, Ciccone and Vickery also concluded that there were no significant differences between the way Summon and EDS performed.[15] Anita Foster and Jean B. MacDonald conducted user studies several years apart on both Summon and EDS, and found that the major differences were in how students behaved when interacting with the different user interfaces.[16] The study had significant methodological flaws, however, including very small research sample sizes, many years between the different studies, and a failure to address changing perceptions of search.

My own research following up on my colleague Jeffrey's "Stress in the workplace" search led me to do a more thorough examination of Summon's algorithmic outputs, first focusing on the results in the Topic Explorer. I inserted a small script on our instance of Summon that checked each time the page loaded to see if there was a Topic Explorer result. If there was, it would save the search string, the Topic Explorer title, source, and content to a database which I could review later. Later, when I began working on this book, I added scripts to capture the results for spelling correction; recommended searches, research guides, and librarians; query expansion; the number of results; and recommended databases.[17]

---

14 Karen Ciccone and John Vickery, "Summon, EBSCO Discovery Service, and Google Scholar: A Comparison of Search Performance Using User Queries," *Evidence Based Library and Information Practice* 10, no. 1 (2015): 39.

15 Ciccone and Vickery, 46.

16 Anita K. Foster and Jean B. MacDonald, "A Tale of Two Discoveries: Comparing the Usability of Summon and EBSCO Discovery Service," *Journal of Web Librarianship* 7, no. 1 (2013): 1–19, https://doi.org/10.1080/193222909.2013.757936.

17 Code for these scripts is available on the GVSU Libraries Github page: https://github.com/gvsulib/Summon-2.0-Scripts.

On the first pass, I selected the first 8,000 of 15,000 searches that were recorded over a 2-month period.[18] I chose 8,000 mainly because it took a long time to manually review each result, and that was about as many as I could get through in the time I had. I was especially interested in the Topic Explorer since it only returns a single result. I first checked to see if the Topic Explorer result was related to the search. Like Ciccone and Vickery at North Carolina State University, my criteria for being on topic was very generous. For instance, a search query for "fetal tissue research" returns the Wikipedia article on "fetus," which is technically on topic but is not useful to the user. Nonetheless, I counted it as relevant. On that first pass, I found that an impressive 93% were topically accurate. But a full 7% were not correct.

Many of these errors fell into predictable categories, although not all. There were topical searches that returned known item entries, like the search for "skin to skin contact" that returned a Wikipedia page for an Australian pop song called "Skin to Skin." Often subject searches returned a Topic Explorer entry for a particular journal, such as the search for "marriage and family" that returns a Wikipedia entry on the "Journal of Marriage and Family." These are at least understandable, if we assume that the algorithm is weighing the keywords in the entry's title more heavily than other factors. More puzzling is the search for "poems," which returned the Gale Virtual Reference Library's article on Ralph Waldo Emerson. While Emerson was a poet, it hardly seemed helpful to introduce the curious user to the entire breadth and history of poetry by offering up a biography of one American writer.

Another group of problems concerned searches for known items. Of these, many returned the wrong known item, usually due to a pattern of words in the titles that was similar. Some examples of this were the searches for "return of the king," where users expected information on the Tolkien novel but instead were shown the Wikipedia entry for a documentary called "The King of Kong: A Fistful of Quarters." Searches for the "city of god" (which could either be a topical or known item search) were shown the page about a non-fiction book called "Farm City: The Education of an Urban Farmer." Many of these known item searches that returned the wrong

---

18   I released these 8,000 searches as a data set. It is available at http://doi.org/10.5281/zenodo.47723.

item concerned journals. Searching for "american journal of transplantation" will get you the "American Journal of Sociology," and the "journal of aquatic sciences" will offer up the "British Journal of Psychiatry." No matter how you search, looking for "the prince" or "the prince machiavelli" would get you research on "Prince, 1958-" the "exciting live performer and prolific singer-songwriter," courtesy of Gale Virtual Reference Library. (And in early 2019, according to all sources in Summon's Topic Explorer, Prince had not died in 2016 of a fentanyl overdose.)

Sometimes a topical search returns topical information, but on the wrong topic. While some combinations seem downright nonsensical ("women are homemakers" returns "sociology"), some can be inadvertently humorous, depending on your political or moral leanings. For instance, searching for "united states healthcare system" returns the Wikipedia article on "United States patent law", which may or may not be a comment on the hold that Big Pharma has on our current healthcare. A search for "princess diana" returns the Gale Virtual Reference Library article on "Wonder Woman." The search for "creation of patriarchy" perhaps rightly introduces the reader to Michelangelo's "Creation of Adam" painting, for if there were to be a starting point of the patriarchy, why not at the beginning? A sad commentary on the rising cost of college tuition might be the search for "united states egg price" which gives us Wikipedia's entry on "Student financial aid in the United States." Those concerned with the influence of sports in our culture will no doubt be pleased to see a search for the "culture of sports" return "the culture of narcissism," and it does seem appropriate to learn more about "legal drugs in the united states" by studying "Public holidays in the United States." Perhaps my favorite, "branding" returns "BDSM," the Wikipedia article for Bondage, Discipline, Sadism, and Masochism dealing with fantasy role play. It's hard not to read that as a statement about corporate image creation.

Indexical bias most often occurred where a search query was matched with an article that implied a social, moral, or political comment on the original search terms. For instance, a search for "corrupt government in united states" returned the Wikipedia entry for "Government procurement in the United States," making the implication that the Government's supply chain is inherently corrupt. Another example was a search for "pollution levels in the usa" which offered the user the Gale Virtual Reference Library article on "Education in the United States." Say what you will, we've had vigorous debates about education in America, but I don't think it's quite reached the point where we can classify it as smog.

Bias cut the other way, at times, such as a search for "history of human trafficking" that returned Wikipedia's entry for the "History of human sexuality," an entry that may be related to trafficking but by no means subsumes the entire topic. A simple search for "history," on the other hand, brings up an entry on the "United States of America," suggesting that the only history that matters is that of the United States.

But more disturbing results came up. A search for "rape in united states," shown in Figure 5.3, returned a Wikipedia article on "Hearsay in United States law," which describes unverified statements made about an event while not under oath. Implying that a search for information on rape in this country is tantamount to searching for unverifiable claims goes beyond merely being incorrect, it reinforces rape culture. A search through the text of the Wikipedia entry on Hearsay shows that the word "rape" never appears in the text.

Initially, the EDS team discovered that searching for "rape in united states" gave an autosuggestion for a search on "race in the united states," a correlation they didn't feel was appropriate (Figure 5.4). According to Eric Frierson, the Director of Field Engineering at EBSCO, the team revisited the autosuggest algorithm to understand why "rape" and "race" were being

Figure 5.3   Summon search for "rape in united states."

Figure 5.4 EDS Search for "rape in united states."

Figure 5.5 EDS Search for "rape myths."

connected.[19] In EDS, a search for "rape myths" returns a Research Starter on "Rape Culture," as shown in Figure 5.5. Likely the research starter was meant to help contextualize the kinds of myths spread by rape culture, but the juxtaposition appears more as an "answer," as Google calls its results. So EDS seems to be implying that "rape culture," the social attitude where rape is normalized, is simply another "myth" about rape.

Other topics seem to support one side of contemporary moral debates, such as a search for "virginity" that produces a Wikipedia entry for "Sexual Abstinence." Virginity and sexual abstinence are not synonymous—you can be sexually abstinent and not be a virgin. Wikipedia has a perfectly

19 Eric Frierson (Director of Field Engineering, North America, EBSCO), phone conversation with author, March 16, 2018.

useful entry on Virginity, and in fact the word virginity only appears on the Sexual abstinence page three times, and two of those are in see also references. In contrast, it appears 121 times in the Virginity entry, including in the title. It appears that the Summon results page expands the default search of "virginity" to include "sexual abstinence" in order to return more results. (Removing that query expansion will return the Wikipedia "Virginity" entry in the Topic Explorer.) While query expansion works well in the case of using synonyms, this query expansion is a different matter. Including the query expansion makes the Topic Explorer entry for sexual abstinence, which has religious and moral overtones, look like a synonym for virginity.

At least a biased result you'd get when searching for "the birth of feminism" has some technical explanation: when you're shown "The Birth of Tragedy," hopefully you'll understand that the algorithm was matching a pattern of words, not comparing feminism with tragedy. Likewise, the "corruption in the army" search that returns the entry on "Women in the military" is matching a pattern in the title and using a synonym: you can try this experiment yourself by putting whatever you like in place of the "x" when visiting GVSU's Summon: "X in the military" will almost always return the Wikipedia entry for "Women in the military," as if the Topic Explorer has become a sort of Mad-Libs. The same pattern is at work with many searches for "women in the," as evidenced by the suggestion that the only role for women in the government is in the military. What's more, when searching for "women in film," the Topic Explorer couldn't

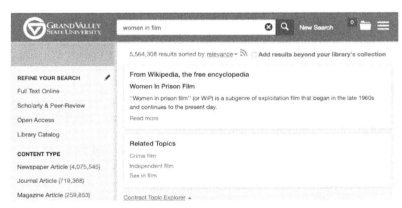

Figure 5.6 Summon search for "women in film."

imagine anything more relevant than the exploitation genre "women in prison films," shown in Figure 5.6.

A search for "domestic violence in the united states" returned the result "domestic partnership in the United States." While domestic partnerships can be between both hetero- and homosexual relationships, the term in popular usage refers to same-sex partnerships. By conflating domestic violence with domestic partnership, the Topic Explorer is undercutting an already marginalized population.

Searching for "muslim terrorist in the united states," shown in Figure 5.7, returned a Wikipedia article on the Islamic religion as a whole. Matching a search for information about terrorists with the entire religion only adds to the stereotypes perpetuated in the aftermath of terrorist attacks of the past few years. This is especially problematic given that Wikipedia itself has an entire entry on Islamic Terrorism (and an entry on Christian Terrorism). Why not bring up the page specifically about terrorism related to that particular religion? The word "terrorist" only appears once in the Islam article, while it appears almost a hundred times in the Islamic Terrorism article. Even "united states" appears 24 times in the Islamic Terrorism entry, while only appearing 5 times in the article on Islam the religion.

While Ex Libris has blocked the Topic Explorer result for "muslim terrorist in the united states," a search for "muslims are" in Summon will activate the autosuggest algorithm as seen in Figure 5.8, which offers only one suggestion: "muslims are terrorists." EDS was a bit more conflicted about the search, suggesting both "muslims are not terrorists" and "muslims are terrorists" (Figure 5.9).

Figure 5.7 Summon search for "muslim terrorist in the united states."

Figure 5.8   Summon search for "muslims are."

Figure 5.9   EDS search for "muslims are."

Searches for "muslim schools in the us" or "islamic schools in the us" return the general entry for "Education in the United States," perhaps suggesting to some that all schools in the United States are Islamic. But this is again an example of naive pattern matching, it seems. Like the earlier Mad Libs searches, you can enter nearly any noun you like into the pattern "X schools in the US" and get this result. This would seem to be more evidence for the additional weight of the title of the topic entry.

If you search in Summon for "white slavery," the Topic Explorer will present you with a Wikipedia entry for "Moral Panic." Searching for "black slavery," meanwhile, returns a blank topic explorer pane, perhaps because Wikipedia itself will offer you nearly 10,000 possible entries related to black slavery. But why is white slavery related to moral panic, while black slavery is not? It's true that the Moral Panic article uses the phrase twice (although one of those is in the references), but Wikipedia itself also has an entry on "White Slavery." How could the algorithm make this kind of a judgment about a topic?

Many searches that involve either crime or race individually will conflate them and show Wikipedia's entry on "Race and crime in the United

States." In the case of a search for a definition of "crime," I'm especially perplexed as to why the Topic Explorer would choose the Race and Crime entry, since Wikipedia's entry "Crime" contains the word "definition" 14 times (although some of those are in use of conceding that it is hard to agree on a consistent definition). But why bring race into question if the user only asked about crime? And why also bring crime into the conversation if the user is asking about race alone? The Wikipedia entry on Race (human categorization) contains a total of six uses of the word crime, although four of them are in "See also" notes. (Race (biology) has no mentions of crime.) This seems to be a case where the algorithm is suggesting possible cross-disciplinary connections, but it does so in a way that amplifies stereotypes. The same can be said of suggesting that poverty is a result of slavery, which is heavily tied up with race. Are we to assume that poor people are still slaves, or that only those whose lineage included being enslaved are poor? The connection is not helpful from a research standpoint, and so we are left trying to make moral or political associations between the topics.

What's more, searching for items of importance to Africa, the continent, tend to default to topics about African-Americans, despite Summon being billed as an international research tool. For instance, in November of 2018, searching for "african history" and "african culture" both returned articles about African-American history and culture. This isn't dependent on GVSU being an American university, either. The result also appeared at the University of Huddersfield in the UK as well as the National University of Singapore, both of which use Wikipedia as a Topic Explorer source. This effectively implies that Africa itself doesn't have a history or culture of its own. Wikipedia has an article on "History of Africa" and "Culture of Africa", each of which can be found by searching Wikipedia natively with the same keywords as the Summon search. (By February 2019, Summon returned Wikipedia articles on African history and culture for these searches.) In another case, a search for "Rastafarianism" returns a fairly accurate Credo entry, but the first sentence lets us know that "rastafarianism is a BLACK religion," setting the racial aspect of the religion for some inexplicable reason in all caps, as if the Topic Explorer is screaming it at us.

Nearly every search I've conducted in Summon that includes the words "Mental Illness," like the one in Figure 5.10, shows the Wikipedia entry for a controversial book by the psychiatrist Thomas Szasz entitled *The Myth of Mental Illness*. Szasz's argument was about the way psychiatry and psychoanalysis were being conducted in the mid-twentieth century, and the

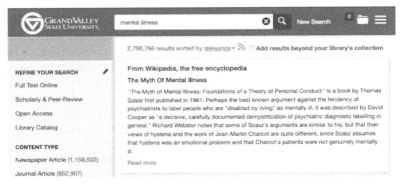

Figure 5.10   Summon search for "mental illness."

title of his book was not intended to suggest that mental illness does not exist. Yet Summon consistently returns this strongly suggestive result whenever users search for topics related to mental illness. Wikipedia itself has a very long and in-depth entry on Mental Disorder, redirected from Mental Illness, which even includes a sentence about the role Szasz played in the development of the legal and psychological understanding of mental illness in the twentieth-century. Yet none of this is presented to Summon users. Rather, any search for mental illness (or, in some cases, just "illness") gives a headline that suggests that the topic they are studying is nothing more than a myth.

In the aftermath of this initial research, Ex Libris moved to make changes to Summon, mostly in the form of blocking offensive results. However, not all problematic results were blocked. As of November 2018, over two and a half years after I shared the results of my research with them (and almost a year after I spoke at a company-wide meeting of ProQuest and Ex Libris engineers)[20], any search for "mental illness" will still show you the Wikipedia entry for "The Myth of Mental Illness." "White slavery" still shows "moral panic," and "virginity" still gets a query expansion for "sexual abstinence."

In the years following my initial research, I have continued to study Summon, incorporating more of its algorithmic outputs, including

---

20   The slides from this talk are available online, at https://mreidsma.github.io/talks/proquest.

examining the lists of search results themselves. But more importantly, I have expanded my examination to other discovery systems. The rest of this chapter will deal with some of the newer results I have found in my research. It should be noted, however, that because I have access to loading customization scripts into Summon, my data collection ability from Summon is much more thorough, and so I may have more examples of problematic results from Summon. This does not necessarily mean that Summon is a more problematic discovery system. What I have been able to do with Summon is allow the system to collect results for me, and then review them. With the other systems, Ex Libris' Primo, EBSCO's EDS, and OCLC's WorldCat Discovery, I had to manually enter in searches that were known to be problematic in Summon and record the results.

Surprisingly, even with this manual process, it wasn't that hard to find biased results. In early 2018, EBSCO offered me access to its EDS service so that I could include it in my analysis of bias in discovery systems. The first searches I ran were those that have tripped up many autosuggest algorithms in the past. I started with "women are," which showed me autosuggest entries for "women are more emotional than men" and "women are weaker than men," in addition to "women are better leaders than men" and two suggestions for known items (Figure 5.11). A search for "immigrants are" showed three results: a book title, a search on whether "immigrants are good for the economy," and the straightforward "immigrants are bad" (Figure 5.12). A search for "asians are" gave me only one suggestion: that "asians are good at math," shown in Figure 5.13.

EDS also has a feature that competes with Summon's Topic Explorer Topics called "Research Starters." Research Starters appear at the top

Figure 5.11   EDS autosuggest for "women are."

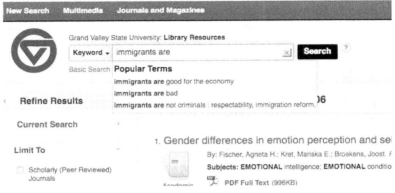

Figure 5.12 EDS autosuggest for "immigrants are."

Figure 5.13 EDS autosuggest for "asians are."

of the results list, and are general guides to understanding a topic, pulled from EBSCO's content sources. I noticed some strange behavior when research starters appeared in some of my searches that I wasn't able to explain. For instance, a search for "slavery" shows a research starter on "Slavery." A search for "white slavery," however, shows a research starter on "Human trafficking," while a search for "black slavery" shows no research starter at all, despite having several entries in the autosuggest algorithm. A search for "african slavery" shows a research starter on "The Slave Trade," which focuses entirely on the United States Slave trade from the 16th through 19th centuries. It seems curious that entries focused on enslaved blacks would refer to the slavery in general terms and focus on the past, while searching for information on white slavery will get you the first mention that the enslaved are "human." This is also a problem, as we saw above, for Summon, which equates "white slavery" with "moral panic."

Another issue with Research Starters is how it treats the idea of racism. A simple search for "racism" returns a research starter on "Scientific racism,"

Grand Valley State University: Library Resources
Keyword
racism
Search
Basic Search
Advanced Search
Search History
Search Results: 1 - 20 of 1,271,436
Relevance
Page Options
Share
Research Starter
"Scientific" racism.
For as long as humans have recognized differences between groups of people, there has been racism in the form of cultural prejudice. In the nineteenth... More
Salem Press Encyclopedia
Other Topics: Racism as an ideology., Racial and ethnic discrimination., Institutional racism.

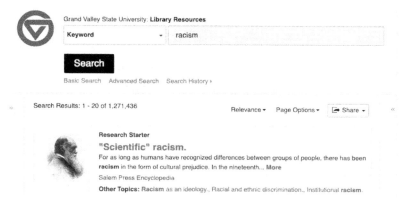

Figure 5.14 EDS Research Starter for the search "racism."

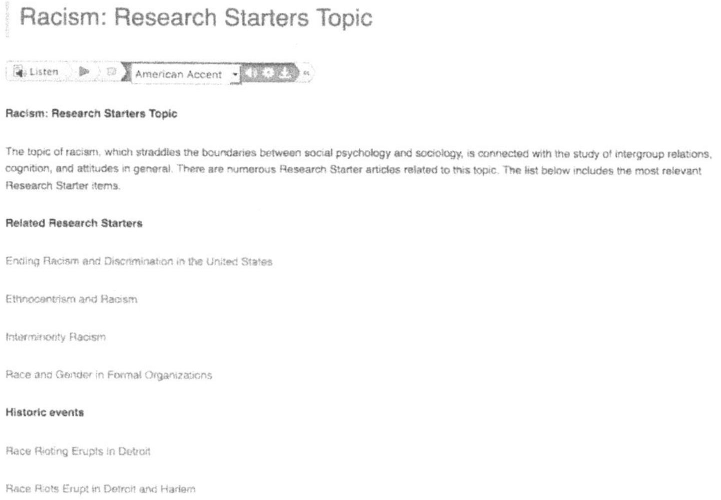

Racism: Research Starters Topic
Listen
American Accent
Racism: Research Starters Topic
The topic of racism, which straddles the boundaries between social psychology and sociology, is connected with the study of intergroup relations, cognition, and attitudes in general. There are numerous Research Starter articles related to this topic. The list below includes the most relevant Research Starter items.
Related Research Starters
Ending Racism and Discrimination in the United States
Ethnocentrism and Racism
Interminority Racism
Race and Gender in Formal Organizations
Historic events
Race Rioting Erupts in Detroit
Race Riots Erupt in Detroit and Harlem

Figure 5.15 EDS Research Starter on Racism.

shown in Figure 5.14, which was the movement in the post-Enlightenment world to apply scientific theory to an understanding of the difference between races. The problem is that a user needs to dive into the research starter entry to fully understand the concept, and why it has long been considered a "bankrupt" theory. What's more, the way the research starter is designed makes it seem like it is equating "racism" with something with the weight of scientific truth. The result isn't the appropriate content for this search. EDS itself has a research starter for "Racism," shown in Figure 5.15, which links to related Research Starters and other topics. (Curiously, the research starter for 'scientific racism' is not one of those listed in the Racism Research Starter.)

EDS's Research Starters struggled in many of the same areas as Summon's Topic Explorer. A search for "sexual misconduct" will give you an entry focused specifically on "sexual misconduct in schools," a more specific topic than was searched. Figure 5.16 shows a search for "sexual harassment," which brings up a Research Starter on the topic that shows an image of Clarence Thomas, the African American Supreme Court Justice who was accused of sexual harassment by Anita Hill during his confirmation hearings in 1991. The juxtaposition of a black man with the topic of sexual harassment is problematic, especially when a similar search for "Sexual Assault" shows a generic EBSCO "Research Starters" image. While a search for "bible" and "the bible" and "holy bible" all returned the same Research Starter for "Bible," the autosuggest for "the bible" suggested "the bible and homosexuality" as the second result, whereas searches for "bible" did not include any suggestions for searches about homosexuality.

EDS's Research Starters and Summon's Topic Explorer are prime subjects for looking for bias, since the algorithms only show you a single result. The implication of these search tools is that they will be correct, and they are picking something that matches your search exactly. Primo and WorldCat Discovery, on the other hand, do not have any such features.

Figure 5.16   EDS Search for "sexual harassment."

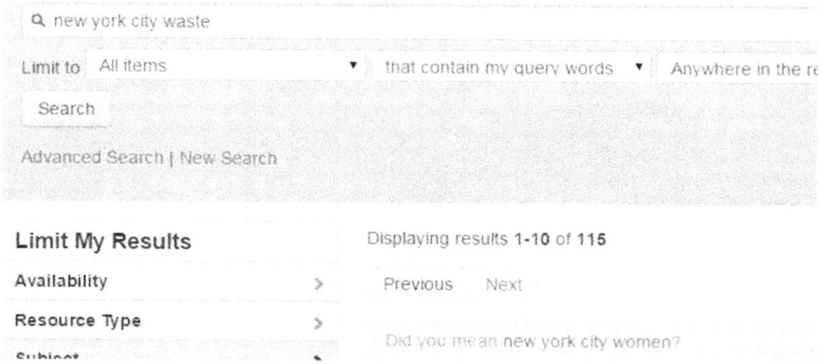

Figure 5.17 Screenshot of Primo search for "new york city waste." Screen shot from *Damn You, Autosuggest.*

Rather, they both display a list of search results with a set of filters for narrowing large results sets, and very few additional algorithms. Neither has, for instance, a database recommender, related searches, librarian or guide recommendations. Both do, however, have autosuggest, which can also be a useful avenue for exploring search tools for bias. In addition, Primo offers an algorithm that attempts to guess what you meant to search for in case of a typo or a low number of results.

Primo's "Did You Mean?" algorithm has undergone a number of improvements over the years, but it began as a fairly aggressive (and notoriously wrong) collection of suggestions. On the website *Damn You, AutoSuggest, or, Primo Knows Best,* a contributor shared a search for "New York City Waste" which Primo thought was really a search for "New York City Women," equating women with trash (Figure 5.17).[21] Nadleen Tempelman-Kluit, the former UX Librarian at New York University Library, shared a suggestion by Primo, shown in Figure 5.18, that a search for "children's literature" should have been a search for "children's sex literature."[22]

21   "Oh, Go to Hell," *Damn You, Autosuggest: Or Primo Knows Best. Auto-Suggest Failures From Library Catalogs and Databases,* March 26, 2015, http://damnyouautosuggest. tumblr.com/post/114699603389/oh-go-to-hell.

22   Nadaleen Tempelman-Kluit, Twitter Post, May 10, 2016, 12:25pm, https://twitter. com/Nadaleen/status/730116596728012800/photo/1.

Figure 5.18   Primo suggestion for search on "children's literature." Screen shot from *Nadaleen Tempelman-Kluit.*

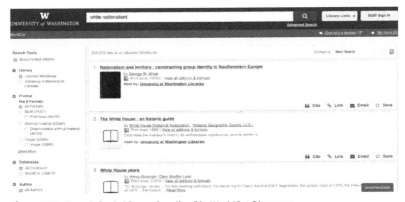

Figure 5.19   Search for "white nationalism" in WorldCat Discovery.

Some results gain different interpretations as events outside of scholarly research develop. For instance, Figure 5.19 shows a search for "white nationalism" in WordCat Discovery. The second result is a monograph on the history of the White House, the literal and symbolic home of the President of the United States. In light of the white nationalist sympathies of current President Donald Trump and his administration, an easily-explained metadata mix-up takes on new meaning. As a colleague said when I showed her the results, "Well, it is wrong, but is it wrong?"

Other algorithms, like those for related topics, also have a tendency to produce problematic results. In one case, shown in Figure 5.20, a search

Figure 5.20 Summon search for "lay investiture." Screen shot by Bob Schoofs.

in Summon for "lay investiture," a query about a practice of the Catholic Church, had related topics for "Fuck" and "Gay." This was quickly suppressed by ProQuest, but it did beg the question of where, exactly, do these "related topics" come from? I can't believe that there is a controlled vocabulary floating around in common use that uses the f-bomb as an authoritative subject heading. Searches for "women in prison" returned the suggested topic "sex in film," again making the connection between women, prison, and sex. A search on the term "murder" suggests a topic on Islamic dietary laws, suggesting that the eating practices of Muslims are perhaps related to homicide. The same related topic appears on a search for "lying to patients," again tying Islam to unethical behavior with no logical connection. "Cocaine addiction" and "pedophilia" are connected to "schizoaffective disorder," despite the mental illness not being related to either of the previous topics in any meaningful way.

The gender bias that comes through in the related searches is as strong as that of the Topic Explorer. A search for "Emily Dickinson," one of the first well-known women poets, has three related topics for white, male poets. A search for information on "violence against women" is connected to the topic "witch hunt," which perhaps initially referred to the historical Salem trials, but more recently has been repurposed by President Donald Trump of the United States to mean a series of false accusations, particularly around his treatment of women.

In Chapter 2, I showed a Summon search for a known item on the information needs of LGBTQ youth, which returned only two results—the item and a compendium on mental illness. The issue here was the limited number of results, and the way the results implied a connection between being gay and mental illness. But problematic search results aren't only limited to situations where there are few results. Consider a search for "9/11" in Summon. Given the holdings at Grand Valley State University, I found it strange that the first result was a pseudo-conspiracy theory book called *9/11: The Simple Facts: Why the Official Story Can't Possibly Be True* (Figure 5.21). Why is this the number one result? There is also a conspiracy theory book owned by GVSU that is the 19th result, meaning that 10% of the top 20 books for this search espouse conspiracy theories about 9/11. What's more, of the eight recommended searches shown in Figure 5.22, fully half are about conspiracies. The Topic Explorer result about the September 11 attacks shown in Figure 5.21 is from Credo Reference, but it was never written to be taken out of context and reads instead like a block of gibberish on the side of the screen.

Taken as a whole, this search results page for basic information on September 11th gives a very different picture than running a search for "September 11" in the exact same search tool, which shows a Topic Explorer result for the Wikipedia article on "September 11," the "first day of the Coptic calendar" (Figure 5.23). There is no mention of the 9/11 attacks. All of the search results are relevant to the September 11th attacks, which

Figure 5.21 Summon search results for "9/11" with Topic Explorer.

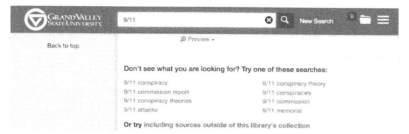

Figure 5.22 Summon recommended searches for search for "9/11."

makes the Topic Explorer result stand out even more. Search for "September 11th" will get you completely different search results, although we still see the Topic Explorer result about the Coptic calendar (Figure 5.24). What are we to make of these radically different results based on small changes in our search terms for a monumentally important topic? Wouldn't this be a good use case for query expansion, which helps tie relevant results together across varied terminology? Why is it that some forms of naming, like 9/11, lend themselves in search results more to emphasizing conspiracies and sowing doubt about the attacks than others?

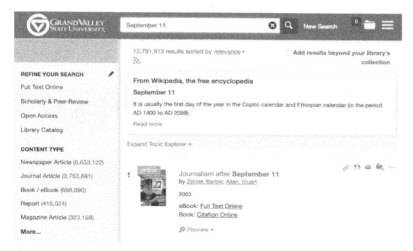

Figure 5.23 Summon search for "September 11."

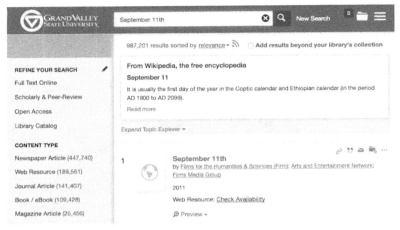

Figure 5.24   Summon search for "September 11th."

It is more common to see these kinds of issues in the algorithms that limit themselves to one or a handful of results, like Summon's Topic Explorer and EDS' Research Starters. And some results straddle the line between merely incorrect and biased. A search for "transgender" in Summon in October 2018 returned a Credo Reference Topic Explorer result for "Transgender, Law," which was effectively a list of legal citations and makes no sense in the Topic Explorer role (Figure 5.25). Why not show the Wikipedia article on transgender, instead of moving towards a legal interpretation?

Figure 5.25   Summon search for "transgender," October 2018.

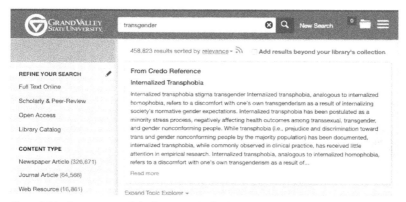

Figure 5.26 Summon search for "transgender," February 4, 2019.

As of early February 2019, this search returned a Credo entry on "Internalized Transphobia," which "refers to discomfort with one's own transgenderism" (Figure 5.26). Why show a result like this that automatically brings up issues of shame and discrimination, rather than an entry on transgenderism itself? What is the impact on users of associating these topics together in a supposedly neutral environment? By February 20, 2019, the result had been updated to show "Transgender Movement," a more appropriate Topic Explorer result.

The Topic Explorer also has a habit of showing results that are based on Western stereotypes. As I mentioned earlier, a search for "history" is given a Topic Explorer result for "The United States of America," as the Credo topic shows (Figure 5.27). A search for "food deserts," which has a terrific Wikipedia article, shows instead a Credo entry for "Agriculture, Cash Crops, Food Security" which begins, "The majority of African nations became independent in the late 1950s and early 1960s" (Figure 5.28). A food desert is any area that has limited access to food, and is primarily used when talking about countries like the United States. So why would Ex Libris use a topic expansion to equate "food desert" with "food scarcity," a more broad term that then implies this is a problem of starvation in Africa? Searching for "famine in africa" will return a query expansion term for "starvation" in Summon, which is perhaps an aspect of famine but by no means a synonym. So a user searching for information on famines in africa will be shown a single result for "Starvation" in the Topic Explorer,

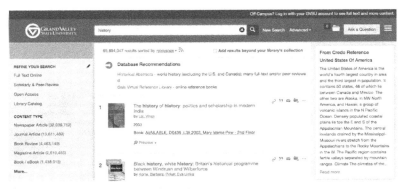

Figure 5.27   Summon search for "history."

Figure 5.28   Summon search for "food desert."

reinforcing the western cultural stereotypes of "starving africans." There is much more to famines than starvation. The western bias of the Topic Explorer limits what users will learn about broad topics that they may be interested in, and shapes their understanding based on assumptions and stereotypes rather than facts. This is the opposite of what the Topic Explorer was supposed to do.

These kinds of careless associations are common with the Topic Explorer, yet tend to affect racial and gender groups that are not white and male. A search for "women in prison," shown in Figure 5.29, returns a

Figure 5.29 Summon search for "women in prison."

Topic Explorer result about "women in prison films," an exploitation genre of film that has very little to do with actual women in actual prisons. And just to be sure you see the connection, a related topic on this same search is "sex in film," despite sharing only a single two-letter word with the original search. (As noted earlier, searching for "women in film" or "sex in film" will also get you this result.)

The Topic Explorer results for searches around alcohol and alcoholism show a strange form of content bias. A search for "alcohol consumption" shows the Credo entry for "alcohol," which is effectively a paragraph on alcohol in prisons: "Prisoners are not allowed to drink," it begins (Figure 5.30). Why immediately tie alcohol consumption to prisoners, when it is a topic that affects the whole population? And why is there a different Credo

Figure 5.30 Summon search for "alcohol consumption."

Figure 5.31   Summon search for "alcohol."

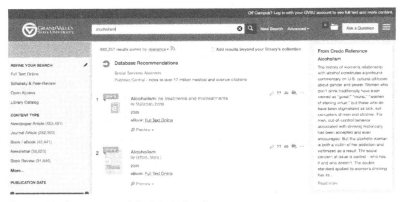

Figure 5.32   Summon search for "alcoholism."

entry entitled "alcohol" for a basic search on the term alcohol, as seen in Figure 5.31? How are these identically named entries chosen? A search for alcoholism also shows a Credo entry for alcoholism, which begins "The history of women's relationship with alcohol constitutes a profound commentary on U.S. cultural attitudes about gender and power" (Figure 5.32). Why tie in a general search about alcoholism with a specific gender? The search wasn't about women alcoholics, it was about alcoholism in general, and showing an entry that talks almost exclusively about women implies that women are or are more likely to be alcoholics.

The Topic Explorer and EDS's Research Starters were created with the intention of creating a perfect algorithm, one that returned only a single result that was guaranteed to match the user's search intentions. As I have shown here, that is not always the case. Yet little has been written about the hubris of this kind of engineering project. Beer describes the engineering goals behind projects like the Topic Explorer and Research Starters, saying that "the search for truth becomes conflated with the perfect algorithms' design—which is to say the search for an algorithm that is seen to make the perfect material intervention."[23] But that is not what these algorithms do. Often, as we have seen, they serve up misleading, incorrect, or biased information. As Stafford Beer famously said, "the purpose of a system is what it does."[24] While library discovery systems do show useful, accurate results in many cases, we cannot keep pretending that this is all they do. It does not matter if the engineering teams did not intend for these biased results to appear—at times this is what library discovery systems do. For now, Primo and WorldCat Discovery seem to be largely immune from these kinds of one-result bias issues, because they do not use many additional algorithms in their systems. Although this may not last long. According to Ex Libris and ProQuest, as reported by librarian Aaron Tay, "Primo will get [some features] from Summon including 'Topic exploration' and 'synonym match'."[25]

For this study, I have reviewed over 20,000 Summon searches, thousands of searches in EBSCO's EDS, and hundreds of searches in Primo and OCLC's WorldCat Discovery. This chapter has just been a small sample of the issues that I found within these tools. Ex Libris' response to reporting issues has been typical of library vendors over my career. They either block the result (without investigating the underlying issues in the algorithm) or they choose to do nothing. Primo, sharing the corporate outlook of the Summon team, also blocks problematic autosuggest results. During my research, only EBSCO's team seemed interested in internally auditing their search algorithms for bias and working to expose the assumptions and

---

23 Beer, "The Social Power of Algorithms," 8.

24 Stafford Beer, "What is Cybernetics?," *Kybernetes,* 31, no. 2 (2002), 217.

25 Aaron Tay, "Primo and Summon—Same but Different?," *Musings About Librarianship* (blog), February 29, 2016, http://musingsaboutlibrarianship.blogspot.com/2016/02/primo-and-summon-same-but-different-i.html.

issues in the algorithm's design that led to the issues. If libraries are going to truly help our users and patrons, we'll need to do more than hope our vendors will take moral leadership of their product's design and upkeep. In the last section of this study, I'll outline some things we can do as a profession to make these tools better for users, including undermining our own claims of objectivity and neutrality.

Chapter 6   Moving Forward

In his book about living in an off-grid cabin in rural North Carolina, the writer William Powers distinguishes between two types of problems: convergent and divergent. Convergent problems are those that have clear answers, "like engineering problems or jigsaw puzzles."[1] Divergent problems are those that afford many approaches and many solutions. Engineers, as Powers notes, prefer convergent problems, and tend to treat all of the issues they face as convergent. Powers sees the irony in this, noting "perhaps a lot of the modern dilemma is that we try to solve divergent problems with convergent logic."[2] This study of library discovery algorithms so far has largely been an examination of what happens when divergent problems are approached by engineers as convergent ones. The unexpected, biased results that appear in seemingly objective search tools are the result of treating everything like a math problem, assigning numerical values to unquantifiable things, of accepting measurable proxies for slippery concepts and ideas.

In this final chapter, I have some suggestions for addressing these issues in our software, aimed at libraries that license software and the teams that build it. Some of these approaches will at first sound like engineering fixes, as if all you need to do to eliminate bias in library discovery is run down the checklist and make sure everything is marked off. But that approach is naïve. The most important step is to recognize that the problems

---

1   William Powers, *Twelve by Twelve: A One-Room Cabin Off the Grid and Beyond the American Dream* (New York: New World Library, 2010), 241.

2   Powers, 241.

with algorithms are not only in the code or the steps of each algorithm; they are not in engineering teams, or the engineering education that leaves out ethical reasoning; they are not in the problematic metadata or the content; they are not even in the business models of the companies that make the algorithms. Rather, the problems can be found only by examining the embedded, historical context in which business practices, engineering education and the lack of diversity, systemic racism and sexism embedded in information classification systems, designs based on prejudiced stereotypes, and a culture that glorifies efficiency above all else. We should not be surprised that our algorithms, created by us and trained on the very inputs and outputs that shape our own biases and prejudices, spit out hate and bias. The question that remains is how can we move forward?

The short answer is that we can't just fix one aspect of the system, for each part depends upon the others. We will not eliminate systemic racism in our search engines while it flourishes elsewhere. We will not see gender equality in our search tools while women and transgender people are systematically made to feel inferior. We cannot hope for equality and equal treatment while the world is such an unequal place. We cannot have an online culture that is so divergent from the offline world. We have to address them all at once, and below I will suggest ways in which libraries can contribute to this healing, specifically addressing library discovery systems.

Recognize the Limitations of Algorithms

As we have seen throughout this book, algorithms work on data that can be enumerated. If it isn't countable, it isn't calculable. If algorithmic designers want to use data that isn't easily quantifiable in their algorithm, they need to either find a way to assign numeric values to the data or find a proxy set of data that could stand in for the data they are hoping to measure. O'Neil showed how credit rating is perhaps one of the most widely used proxies, where your financial ranking is used to stand in for your trustworthiness as a tenant or your suitability as an employee.[3] But these proxies don't measure what they claim to measure, and often give inaccurate or misleading results.

---

3   O'Neil, *Weapons of Math Destruction*, 8.

Proxies aren't always bad. When GVSU moved into our new Mary Idema Pew Library Learning and Information Commons in 2013, administration wanted to know which floor was the busiest, and explored installing sensors or sending students out to do exact counts of people at 15 minute increments. Since the need for exact numbers wasn't important, I suggested instead that we just record the readings on the water bottle refill station displays, which tallied "number of water bottles saved." The floor with the greatest water station use would probably correlate to the busiest floor. (The third floor, which has the quiet reading room, was the landslide winner of the busiest floor.) This proxy worked for us because we didn't need an exact measurement of how many people were using each floor and because the stakes were very low. We weren't using the data to allocate funds or resources to each floor—we mostly wondered how the spaces we had designed were being used. Later, we also used other proxies to better measure usage, including lab computer usage and head counts. (The third floor still came out on top.)

But even these proxies can't tell us for sure that the third floor is the busiest floor. The third floor could just be full of very thirsty people. In fact, the third floor is home to our technical services staff, who mostly work at their desks all day. The second and fourth floors are home to the liaison librarians and administration, respectively, who take more meetings, especially outside of the library, than the third floor staff. The water bottle numbers could have been skewed by over a dozen staff who are mostly at their desks refilling their water bottles all day, while the other staff were in other buildings, using other water bottle refill stations. That was one reason we correlated the data with other proxies and with actual head counts.

The point is, using proxy data will not make an accurate algorithm. But even using directly measurable data might not make your algorithm perfect. Many of the factors we want to measure, such as relevance, are not easily quantifiable. And because the creators of the algorithms have their own values and biases, unexpected results are practically inevitable. (The irony is that both Microsoft and Facebook, who each have abysmal track records on algorithmic bias, are creating algorithms to root out algorithmic bias, as we saw in Chapter 4.[4] Do we trust that the biased developers who

---

4   Wiggers, "Microsoft Is Developing a Tool to Help Engineers Catch Bias in Algorithms;" Gershgorn, "Facebook Says It Has a Tool to Detect Bias in Its Artificial Intelligence."

created biased algorithms will be able to create unbiased algorithms to detect their own bias?)

The best way we can approach these issues is to retract some of the faith we have in algorithms. The trust that we have blindly handed them is not deserved. One of the reasons that there are fewer instances of biased Primo and WorldCat Discovery searches in Chapter 5 is that these systems do not have the overconfidence to create algorithms that show only a single result, like Summon's Topic Explorer or EDS's Research Starters. They still have problems, but the vast majority of the issues I have uncovered involve the hubris of trusting an algorithmic system to determine, based on very few hastily-typed keywords, what a person wants or needs. If you are designing or licensing a third-party search tool, avoiding or turning off these features will go a long way in avoiding biased results for library users.

Stop Focusing on Tools

In their 1999 book, *Information Ecologies: Using Technology With Heart*, MIT researchers Bonnie Nardi and Vicki O'Day point out that we engage with the world largely through metaphor. By using metaphors, we highlight certain aspects of the new experience or thing that is like another experience or thing we already know. But we also cut off ourselves from the aspects that are different from the metaphor. We think frog legs taste like chicken, even though they might taste very much like something else. And we understand arguments as wars, although we could also understand them as diplomacy.

For Nardi and O'Day, the most common metaphor for technology is as a tool.[5] We think of technologies as things that have a separate existence outside of the people that create them and use them, and that structures how we design them. Because we see technologies strictly as tools, we ignore the social and moral elements of designing them, since by necessity technologies are only useful when used. While the tool metaphor is great for helping us understand some aspects of technology (the functional aspects, in particular) by limiting our view of technology to that of a mere

---

5   Bonnie A. Nardi, Vicki L. O'Day, *Information Ecologies: Using Technology With Heart* (Cambridge, MA: MIT Press, 1999), 27–28.

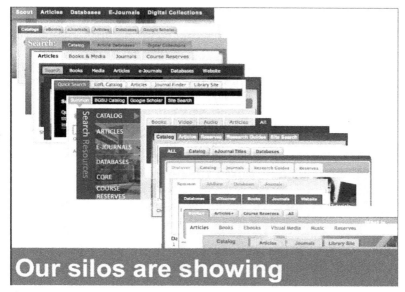

Figure 6.1 Erin White's slide showing library search tools that mirror functional silos.

tool, we cut ourselves off from the embeddedness of the technological creations we make. It becomes much harder to understand how a programming language, the upbringing and demographics of an engineering team, the workplace culture of a software company, the current political and cultural climate of users, and the actual life experiences of people who will use the technology intersect in the creation and use of any given technology.

We see this a lot in libraries. Erin White, the Head of Digital Engagement at Virginia Commonwealth University Libraries, has a slide in her 2012 talk, "Data-Driven Design Decisions for Discovery Interfaces," shown in Figure 6.1, that highlights how the focus in libraries on tools isn't limited to technology-focused librarians.[6] Rather, the very structures of our organizations are siloed to intersect with the particular functional

---

6   Erin White, "Data-Driven Design Decisions for Discovery Interfaces," *LITA Forum 2012, Columbus, OH*, October 6, 2012, https://scholarscompass.vcu.edu/cgi/viewcontent.cgi?article=1006&context=libraries_present.

tool-based workflows we find important. "Our silos are showing," she quips below a collection of screenshots of library search tools, all broken down by functional silo: monographs, serials, and electronic resources.

Nardi and O'Day recommend a more useful metaphor for understanding technology: an information ecology. An information ecology is a "system of people, practices, values, and technologies in a particular local environment".[7] The ecology metaphor does a much better job of tying together all the different aspects of the world that come together to influence the creation and use of technology than the tool metaphor. A hospital intensive care unit is a great example of an information ecology. "It has an impressive collection of people and technologies, all focused on the activity of treating critically ill patients."[8] A library is also an information ecology.

Nardi and O'Day use a library as an example of an information ecology, arguing that librarians are a "keystone species," a population whose survival is essential to a healthy ecosystem.[9] In a library, you have librarians, users, databases, books, indices, newspapers, microfilm, computers, professional values, a culture of learning, and coffee, all interacting in a big, messy way.

The thing about the ecology metaphor is that it highlights the interconnectedness of all of these different things coming together in one place. It emphasizes the co-evolution of technology and people. Its about people and tools together.

Perhaps the most useful reason for dropping the tool metaphor is that tools require convergent thinking. You cannot create a tool with divergent thinking, where many possibilities exist. That's why you don't see tools that have wildly different shapes. You might find a selection of two dozen hammers in the hardware store, and each may have some slight innovation or difference that gives it an edge over its competitors, but they will all basically look like a hammer. Engineers have settled on the most efficient, basic form of a tool for pounding nails into boards, and it looks like a hammer. And that is what convergent thinking is great for. This is also why nearly every search tool looks remarkably like Google, because the focus on search as

---

7 Nardi and O'Day, *Information Ecologies,* 49.

8 Nardi and O'Day, 49.

9 Nardi and O'Day, 79–81.

a "tool" keeps the focus on the existing workflows and processes that have characterized other search tools. But we don't do a very good job of thinking about the interconnectedness of all of our systems when we get stuck in task-based, convergent thinking.

Rather, by switching our focus to seeing our technological systems as ecologies, and thus using divergent thinking to address the design and engineering of these systems, we can move beyond the limitations of tool-based thinking and design systems that are made to be used by diverse people who are embedded within particular social, cultural, and historical contexts. Even when we design tools and conduct usability tests to see how users interact with them, the focus is always on the tool itself: Is it intuitive? Is the wording clear? Can we reduce friction? The focus on the usability of the tool further divorces the tool from the users' and the creators' worlds, and assumes that the tool is a stand-alone artifact that isn't shaped by the worldviews, beliefs, and values of its creators or interpreted, changed, and shaped by those who use it. No technology exists in a vacuum, but the current focus on tools, and the corollary focus on "usability" being all about the tool, leads us to design and build tools that are for use in vacuums.

Ethnography

Currently, the move in libraries to focusing on user experience has made many improvements for our users, as designers and engineers focus more on the experience of using their tools. But often this focus on "the user" is less about the actual people using the tools and more about the assumptions of the engineering team. Many of the user experience articles that are currently flooding library publications are about teams trying to confirm hypotheses or assumptions, rather than truly trying to learn how their users work and how to help them do research. And this isn't limited to libraries. Wachter-Boettcher writes about Fatima, a designer who formerly worked for a major technology company and who witnessed a failed smartwatch design for women that was based not on actual user research. "It wasn't based on needs," she said, "it was based on stereotypes."[10] Wachter-Boettcher goes on to examine the main assumption behind many "user experience" projects:

---

10 Wachter-Boettcher, *Technically Wrong*, 15.

that there is such a thing as an "average user."[11] The idea is that a significant percentage of users will use your product in the same way. That is, regardless of the time of day, their stage of life, whether they are tired or angry or hungry or scared, they will interact with your tool or service in exactly the same way. Eric Meyer and Wachter-Boettcher examined this same issue, noting that designers rarely "look beyond that ideal persona, in that ideal circumstance, and ask, 'how will someone in another context perceive this?' ... We work from an imagined ideal, both in terms of the user and the user experience."[12] A cursory examination of your own experience using technology over the past 24 hours will probably give the lie to this assumption. As Mailchimp content strategist Katie Keifer Lee said, "our readers and customers are people. They could be in an emergency and they still have to use the internet."[13] Just because we work "only in libraries" doesn't mean that our users will not come to us in moments of crisis. I know of patrons who have used library chat services when they are feeling suicidal, and countless youth who are struggling with identity and gender feelings that come to the library to help make sense of their lives. But, at other times, they may come for a leisure read. As Whitman famously wrote, "very well, then, I contradict myself; (I am large—I contain multitudes.)"[14] The idea of an "average" user isn't sustainable, or helpful.

What's more, much of this "user research" is not designed to solve actual user problems, but to conflate business strategies with user needs. Roger McNamee, a venture capitalist, pointed out that "Facebook and Google assert with merit that they are giving users what they want. The same can be said about tobacco companies and drug dealers."[15] The problem is that

---

11   Wachter-Boettcher, 38.

12   Eric Meyer and Sara Wachter-Boettcher, *Design for Real Life* (New York: A Book Apart, 2016), 9.

13   Wachter-Boettcher, *Technically Wrong,* 90.

14   Walt Whitman, "Leaves of Grass," *Bartleby.com,* accessed February 21, 2019, https://www.bartleby.com/142/14.html.

15   Paul Lewis, "'Our Minds Can Be Hijacked': The Tech Insiders Who Fear a Smartphone Dystopia," *The Guardian,* October 6, 2017, https://www.theguardian.com/technology/2017/oct/05/smartphone-addiction-silicon-valley-dystopia.

often what the users want doesn't align with what benefits the company most. Tristan Harris, a former ethicist at Google, notes that

> People in tech will say, "You told me, when I asked you what you wanted, that you wanted to go to the gym. That's what you said. But then I handed you a box of doughnuts and you went for the doughnuts, so that must be what you really wanted." The Facebook folks, that's literally what they think. We offer people this other stuff, but then they always go for the outrage, or the autoplaying video, and that must be people's most true preference.[16]

We see this time and again in user experience work, where the idea of experience or needs or wants, something that is not even remotely quantifiable, is replaced by easily enumerated proxies, like page views or clicks. Donna Lanclos and Andrew Asher, anthropologists who work in libraries, write that "the overarching perception around assessment in libraries is that quantitative work gives effective (occasionally easy) benchmarks, and is generally a way to measure success and satisfaction."[17] Harris points out that design teams often interpret these data trails as the true desires of the users, when they really have none of the actual context of someone's life to make sense of the real reasons behind any of this behavioral data. He emphasizes the disconnect between wants and needs on the one hand, and behaviors on the other: "I think the [traffic] metrics have created this whole illusion that what people are doing is what people want, when it's really just what works in the moment, in that situation."[18]

User Experience research done in libraries and by library software vendors often focuses on testing existing software to see if it is usable by users, rather than doing ethnographic research into the actual needs of a user community. (Lanclos and Asher refer to this kind of research as

---

16   Ezra Klein, "How Technology Is Designed to Bring Out the Worst in Us," *Vox*, February 19, 2018, https://www.vox.com/technology/2018/2/19/17020310/tristan-harris-facebook-twitter-humane-tech-time.

17   Donna Lanclos and Andrew Asher, "'Ethnographish': The State of the Ethnography in Libraries," *Weave Journal of Library User Experience* 1, no. 5 (October 2016), http://dx.doi.org/10.3998/weave.12535642.0001.503.

18   Klein, "How Technology Is Designed to Bring Out the Worst in Us."

"ethnographish," rather than ethnographic.[19]) By ignoring these long-term ethnography projects, libraries and software vendors are missing a key component to designing tools and services for actual people. As designer Erica Hall reminds us, "design happens in context. And research is simply understanding that context."[20] It is essential for us to work to understand the human lives and needs and wants of our users before we begin creating services and tools, so that we have a better understanding of our audience and we don't end up designing for stereotypes or assumptions.

But the research we conduct to evaluate our existing tools is just as important, and must go farther than just checking to see if the buttons are big enough or if our users are confused by a label. As the Dutch researchers Engin Bozdag and Ibo van de Poel argue,

> information technology is a constitutive technology, so that it shapes
> our discourses, practices and institutions and experiences in import-
> ant ways … technological artifacts and systems function much like
> laws, by constraining behavior and serving as frameworks for pub-
> lic order."[21]

By creating and purchasing software tools, we are shaping the behavior and possibilities of our users, and those kinds of choices by necessity have moral implications. The philosopher of technology, Peter-Paul Verbeek, argues that "artifacts are morally charged; they mediate moral decisions, shape moral subjects, and play an important role in moral agency."[22] Verbeek further argues that you cannot separate out the human users and the technological artifact. "Humans are technological beings, just as technologies are social entities."[23] Technologies, in their very use, change the context in

---

19 Lanclos and Asher, "'Ethnographish'."

20 Hall, *Just Enough Research,* 22.

21 Engin Bozdag and Ibo van de Poel, "Designing for Diversity in Online News Rec-
    ommenders," *2013 Proceedings of PICMET '13: Technology Management for Emerging
    Technolgies,* (2013): 1102.

22 Peter-Paul Verbeek, *Moralizing Technology: Understanding and Designing the Morality
    of Things* (Chicago: University of Chicago Press, 2011), 21.

23 Verbeek, *Moralizing Technology,* 4.

which they function. We must focus not merely on the tool, as we often do now, and not merely on the user, but on "mediation,"[24] as Verbeek puts it, "the point where the artifact and human subjectivity come together to create effects that cannot be located in either the artifact or the subject taken alone."[25]

By digging deep into the lived experience of our users and reflecting on what we learn when building and licensing tools, we will be more aware of the subtle (and at times, not so subtle) biases that plague our library systems, tools, and services. As Lanclos and Asher propose, libraries need to engage more in ethnographic practices, but with an eye toward understanding, not quantifying. "Ethnography should not be engaged in simply as a method that gives us more buckets of data to be sorted, visualized, and put into a report. Ethnography should be core to the business of the library."[26]

Design

In the past few years, the ethical implications of Big Tech's design methods have been front and center: Social media's role in the misinformation campaign during the 2016 US elections; Facebook's questionable data practices, exposed by enormous breeches and suspect business arrangements; technology companies' policies that violated federal laws and turned racist and anti-semitic views into a marketing strategy; Google's true business model, marketing data about all of its users to enrich its shareholders; and the race to put self-driving cars on the road, which has led to the death of a pedestrian in Arizona.

One reason for these revelations is that these companies approach every aspect of their work like an engineering problem. Facebook is notorious for this, according to Wachter-Boettcher, having "a long track record of treating ethical failures like bugs to be fixed ... every failure gets treated like an isolated incident, rather than part of a systemic pattern that needs

---

24   Verbeek, 7–8.

25   Sacasas, "The Ethics of Technological Mediation."

26   Lanclos and Asher, "'Ethnographish'."

systemic action."[27] Rather than ask how its workplace culture or its infamous motto, "move fast and break things," might be contributing to these ethical failures, Facebook reacts to each new crisis as if it were the first, tossing out weak patches to give the appearance of due diligence. But this kind of focus on individual decisions doesn't leave room for a wholesale ethical framework when creating services and tools. For instance, in 2016 *Fast Company* reported that Mercedes Benz' self-driving car algorithms were programmed to always save the car's driver and the passengers in a crash situation.[28] This caused some outrage, but would it have been better for the designers to instead always choose to save the occupants of another car or pedestrians? Who would buy that car? Rather, the problem is in how this entire scenario was approached, as if an ethical decision like this can be made without context, in one sweeping action that will apply to every situation.

These ethical problems are approached with the same set of tools that engineers and designers use to choose palette colors or design circuits for everyday objects. Broussard points out that these everyday objects often fail to live up to the promises made by those who have designed them. "The little things like elevators and automatic faucets matter because they are indicators of the functioning of a larger system. Unless the little things work, it's naive to assume the bigger issues will magically work."[29] O'Neil points out that in designing systems "we're often faced with a choice between fairness and efficacy."[30] Our judicial system tends to favor fairness, "so the system sacrifices enormous efficiencies for the promise of fairness."[31] Engineering culture, on the other hand, favors efficiency. Efficiency can be easily measured, but "fairness is squishy and hard to quantify. It is a concept ...

---

27   Wachter-Boettcher, "Facebook Treats Its Ethical Failures Like Software Bugs, and That's Why They Keep Happening."

28   Charlie Sorrel, "Self-Driving Mercedes Will Be Programmed To Sacrifice Pedestrians To Save The Driver," *Fast Company,* October 13, 2016, https://www.fastcompany.com/3064539/self-driving-mercedes-will-be-programmed-to-sacrifice-pedestrians-to-save-the-driver.

29   Broussard, *Artificial Unintelligence,* 157.

30   O'Neil, *Weapons of Math Destruction,* 95.

31   O'Neil, 95.

So fairness isn't calculated into [algorithms]. And the result is massive, industrial production of unfairness."[32] To remedy this, she argues, sometimes companies will need to put fairness ahead of efficiency (and profit) by building explicit values right into their algorithmic systems.[33]

Designers have also exploited our psychological vulnerabilities in their technological designs. One simple example is the little red notification badge on apps that was developed by engineer Chris Marcellino at Apple. These badges show the number of unread messages or emails or notifications, and are red because eye tracking studies have shown that people will focus more quickly on warm colors like reds. What's more, these notifications were designed explicitly to get users to interact more with the apps and devices. Says Marcellino, "it is not inherently evil to bring people back to your product. It's capitalism."[34]

In the library software world, these tricks are found in the deceitful ways that the vendors win our trust. Arguing that their results are objective and up-to-date while designing algorithms that show out-of-date Wikipedia entries for common searches while claiming in their documentation to be updating records regularly. Playing off librarian anxieties about "relevance" and "objectivity" to sell annual licenses to discovery systems that prioritize content from the same vendor's subscription databases. So how do we move beyond these unethical design practices?

Designer and author Stephen P. Anderson reminds us that "all design influences behavior, even if we're not intentional about the desired behaviors."[35] Keeping this simple fact in mind when we are designing services and tools is a first step—each choice we make will influence how someone else will behave, often in a context very different from our own. Library software developer Bess Sadler and Director of the MIT Libraries Chris Bourg suggest approaching the design processes from a place of advocacy, which "asks how we can design systems that improve users' lives without imposing

---

32   O'Neil, 95.

33   O'Neil, 204.

34   Lewis, "'Our Minds Can Be Hijacked'."

35   Stephen P. Anderson, "Towards an Ethics of Persuasion," *Ux Mag,* December 13, 2011, http://uxmag.com/articles/towards-an-ethics-of-persuasion.

the designer's view of what might constitute an improvement."[36] This, of course, requires us to be engaged in ethnography, to understand the lives and needs of our users. But it also helps us reflect on our own biases as designers. Broussard recommends that we "assume discrimination is the default, then we can design systems that work toward notions of equality."[37] And Wachter-Boettcher recommends that designers move away from their flawed notions of the "average user" and "edge case," to begin focusing on the context our users find themselves in, especially when that context finds users in a stressful situation. "When designers call someone an edge case, they imply that they're not important enough to care about—that they're outside the bounds of concern. In contrast, a stress case shows designers how strong their work is—and where it breaks down."[38]

Bozdag and van de Poel recommend Value Sensitive Design (VSD), which "is an approach that aims to integrate values and ethical importance in a principled and comprehensive manner into the design of information technology."[39] Practitioners of VSD make the values and ethical stances they hope their products will embody explicit during the design process, just like other design and technical requirements. They then target those ethical goals in the same manner they target design and engineering goals. Eubanks, recognizing that it is easier for individuals to change their approach than for entire teams to shift to a new way of working together, created an "Oath of Non-Harm for an Age of Big Data."[40] Although targeted at data scientists, many of the precepts help designers and engineers incorporate ethical inquiry into their daily work, such as:

· I will remember that technologies I design are not aimed at data points, probabilities, or patterns, but at human beings.

· I will not use my technical knowledge to compound the disadvantages created by historic patterns of racism, classism, able-ism, sexism,

---

36   Sadler and Bourg, "Feminism and the Future of Library Discovery."

37   Broussard, *Artificial Unintelligence,* 150.

38   Wachter-Boettcher, *Technically Wrong,* 40.

39   Bozdag and van de Poel, "Designing for Diversity in Online News Recommenders," 1103.

40   Eubanks, *Automating Inequality,* 212–13.

homophobia, xenophobia, transphobia, religious intolerance, and other forms of oppression.

· I will design with history in mind. To ignore a four-century-long pattern of punishing the poor is to be complicit in the 'unintended' but terribly predictable consequences that arise when equity and good intentions are assumed as initial conditions.[41]

Infrastructure and Staffing

One other drawback to the focus on technology as a tool rather than as an ecology is that it is easy to assume that isolated tools are inherently neutral, and any moral or ethical issues that arise with tool use are due to how the technology is *used* by people. But Langdon Winner, the Thomas Phelan Chair of Humanities and Social Sciences at Rensselaer Polytechnic Institute, has shown that technologies always reflect the human values that lie behind their design and creation. For instance, nuclear power plants reflect the values of centralized control over energy production, while solar power is reflective of a decentralized, communal approach to producing energy.[42] Far from being "neutral" tools for energy production, nuclear and solar are reflective of the competing values of their creators and proponents. Noble, talking about Winner's work, notes that "the more we can make transparent the political dimensions of technology, the more we might be able to intervene in the spaces where algorithms are becoming a substitute for public policy debates over resource distribution."[43] Engineers and designers, as well as librarians who use these tools and have a say in the licensing and purchase of software, need to work to make these values more explicit. Often the people who designed and built a tool haven't thought carefully about the values that shaped their work. They often intended to embed

---

41 Eubanks, 212–13.

42 Langdon Winner, "Do Artifacts Have Politics?," *Daedalus* 109, no. 1 (1980): 130.

43 Noble, *Algorithms of Oppression*, 90.

altruistic values into their work, while their own unexamined assumptions take the work in a different direction.

For instance, the engineers at Summon no doubt wanted to embed the values of independence and curiosity into their Topic Explorer algorithm, showing novice searchers contextual information to help them better understand their topic. Instead, through infrastructure decisions involving where data lives and how it is indexed, they have created a tool for potentially showing out-of-date information laced with racial, gender, and other biases. While not all of the ethical problems inherent in Summon's Topic Explorer would be solved by better infrastructure choices, many would be improved. Coupled with these infrastructure choices is the lack of understanding of the tool that is being built. Conger and Metz share the story of Jack Poulson, a former engineer at Google. "Most people don't know the holistic scope of what they're building. You don't have knowledge of where it's going unless you're sufficiently senior."[44] Often engineers and designers are working on a small fraction of a system or even feature, and are unable to fully see how the work they do will integrate into a whole. This is a recipe for functional and ethical blind spots, and the results can be seen in library software every day. But it doesn't have to be that way. Wachter-Boettcher implores us that "regardless of the makeup of the team behind an algorithmically powered product, people must be trained to think more carefully about the data they're working with, and the historical context of that data."[45]

This brings us to the uncomfortable fact that most software engineers working today are white males.[46] Joy Buolamwini, working in the MIT Media Lab on why facial recognition technology favors light-skinned faces, succinctly states "who codes matters."[47] Librarianship is also a white-dominated profession according to the American Library Association, with 88% of credentialed librarians in 2010 self-reporting as white.[48] This lack

44 Conger and Metz, "Tech Workers Now Want to Know."

45 Wachter-Boettcher, *Technically Wrong*, 136.

46 Laszlo Block, "Getting to Work on Diversity at Google," *Google Official Blog*, May 28, 2014, https://googleblog.blogspot.com/2014/05/getting-to-work-on-diversity-at-google.html.

47 Buolamwini, "How I'm Fighting Bias in Algorithms."

48 "Diversity Counts," *American Library Association*, 2012, http://www.ala.org/aboutala/offices/diversity/diversitycounts/divcounts.

of diversity in libraries and software engineering teams hurts us all. There are some promising programs to increase the diversity of the field, such as ACRL's Diversity Fellowships, but more needs to be done to specifically recruit diverse developers and designers to create the software that libraries run on today. It's easy to assume that even with the skewed demographics of the profession, that many librarians and library staff support diversity initiatives and values such as those in the IFLA or ALA Codes of Ethics.[49]

But this by no means means that all developers working on library software welcome these initiatives. At the Code4Lib 2018 National Conference in Washington, D.C., keynote speaker Chris Bourg highlighted research into many of the roadblocks that stand in the way of increasing diversity in the technology sector,[50] like the "Tech Leavers Study."[51] According to a statement released by Code4Lib, Bourg "has been subjected to widespread and coordinated harassment across several platforms, including homophobic and sexist personal attacks, as well as commentary that discounts her expertise, ignores the nuances of her argument, and misrepresents her position."[52] That her keynote at a library-specific function was met by a wave of attacks from technology generalists suggests that there were those in the audience at Code4Lib—a conference composed primarily of library technologists—who did not agree with Bourg's message of diversity and inclusion. While many of the critiques in this book have been aimed at inadvertent actions by otherwise well-meaning developers and designers, we must also be mindful that not everyone working within libraries shares these values. And that makes it all the more important that we

---

49 American Library Association, "Professional Ethics"; "Professional Codes of Ethics for Librarians," *IFLA,* June 15, 2017, https://www.ifla.org/faife/professional-codes-of-ethics-for-librarians.

50 Chris Bourg, "For the Love of Baby Unicorns," Keynote address at Code4Lib National Conference, February 14, 2018, https://2018.code4lib.org/keynotes/Chris-Bourg.

51 Allison Scott, Freada Kapor Klein, and Uriridiakoghene Onovakpuri, "Tech Leavers Study: A First-Of-Its-Kind Analysis of Why People Voluntarily Left Jobs in Tech," *The Kapor Center for Social Impact,* April 27, 2017, https://www.kaporcenter.org/wp-content/uploads/2017/08/TechLeavers2017.pdf.

52 "Code4Lib Community Statement in Support of Chris Bourg," *Github: Code4Lib,* accessed February 21, 2019, https://github.com/code4lib/c4l18-keynote-statement.

consciously embed library values of inclusion and diversity into the tools and services we create.

Since library values emphasize the importance of open access content and sharing, it is not surprising that many library software projects are open source, allowing community members to contribute to and modify the code either for their own uses or to improve the product for others. This would seem to be a salve for the problems of black-boxed algorithmic systems, for by putting the code out in the open to be evaluated and revised by the community, bias could hopefully be identified and removed. But this assumes that bias can be seen by looking at code, without access to the assumptions of the authors. The diversity of open source projects teams is even more problematic than the general library technology population. According to Dawn Nafus, Bernhard Krieger, and James Leach, only around two percent of software developers working on open source projects are women.[53] And Sadler and Bourg note that "the open source community is also a notoriously sexist space, as documented in the Twitter feeds of many women software engineers and in academic papers such as 'Free as in Sexist: Free culture and the gender gap' by Joseph Reagle."[54]

One additional reason we leave the moral and ethical responsibilities of technology creators unexamined is the role that technology plays in our culture. Technology is seen as close to magic, something to be made and tamed by an elite class of developers who are blessed with abilities we cannot comprehend. This is especially evident in libraries, where a relatively small percentage of the workforce creates and manages software, yet every professional publication contains at least one article arguing that everyone who works in a library needs to be able to write code. But writing code, planning software, and designing tools and services is, as Wachter-Boettcher reminds us, "just a skill set—one that all kinds of people can, and do, learn."[55] It is not magic. We cannot move forward in examining the values in our existing tools without first shedding these assumptions about the

---

53 Dawn Nafus, Bernhard Kreiger, and James Leach, "Gender: Integrated Report of Findings," *Free/Libre and Open Source Software: Policy Support,* March 1, 2006, http://flosspols.merit.unu.edu/deliverables/FLOSSPOLS-D16-Gender_Integrated_Report_of_Findings.pdf, 4.

54 Sadler and Bourg, "Feminism and the Future of Library Discovery."

55 Wachter-Boettcher, *Technically Wrong,* 26.

magical abilities of engineers and designers. You don't need to know how to write code to see that the Google results Noble saw when searching for "black girls" were both racist and sexist. You do not need a degree in computer science to see the dangers inherent in allowing a computer to decide, based on one or two keywords, exactly what the user wants. Those who do not or cannot write code can still critically examine the tools of our profession and share what they've learned. According to Eubanks, this skill is as important as writing better code: "the best cure for the misuse of big data [and algorithms] is telling better stories."[56]

We can all examine the software tools that we use every day by running audits and sharing what we learn. In Chapter 5, I showed a few examples of search results that were reported to me by users or fellow librarians who stumbled across problematic or biased results. But the majority of the issues I have looked at (and the hundreds that did not make the book) were found by intentionally auditing our software tools. Simonite notes that to find bias in algorithmic systems "requires a researcher to be looking for bias in the first place."[57] While some companies no doubt conduct internal bias audits, O'Neil reminds us that this helps companies "shield their algorithms inner workings, and its prejudices, from outsiders. But insiders, suffering as we do from confirmation bias, are more likely to see what they expect to find."[58]

There is certainly room for more accountability and investigation within software teams. The technology industry in general is paying more attention to this, as algorithmic scandals make up more of our daily news cycle. Anne Wojcicki, the CEO of the DNA testing company 23andMe, argued against hiring a single person to focus on the ethical issues of software, saying "it has to be our management and leaders who have to add this [ethics] to their skillset, rather than just hire one person to determine this."[59] But we cannot leave the examination of algorithmic systems only to their

---

56   Eubanks, *Automating Inequality,* 205.

57   Simonite, "Machines Taught by Photos Learn a Sexist View of Women."

58   O'Neil, *Weapons of Math Destruction,* 212.

59   Kara Swisher, "Who Will Teach Silicon Valley to Be Ethical?," *New York Times,* October 21, 2018, https://www.nytimes.com/2018/10/21/opinion/who-will-teach-silicon-valley-to-be-ethical.html.

creators. The incentive to use algorithms that prove effective despite shaky ethical underpinnings is too great. Lohr felt compelled to make this explicit, noting that it went against the common business practices of software companies: "just because an algorithm finds a correlation, that doesn't necessarily mean you should exploit it."[60]

O'Neil suggests that starting any audit is to assume that the algorithm is a "black box that takes in data and spits out conclusions. ... By studying these outputs, we could piece together the assumptions behind the model and score them for fairness."[61] As we have seen, this is a complicated process, especially in search, since each vendor will have different criteria for how they index, match, and rank results. This makes studies like this one, which look across a variety of vendors, much more difficult. Kerstin Denecke, a professor at Bern University of Applied Sciences, notes that the variety of matching and ranking criteria "results in totally different search results, and in turn, in a great challenge in evaluating the performance of information retrieval systems."[62]

Teaching

Finally, we have a responsibility to better educate those who create these systems, those of us in the library who build and license them, and our users who often assume that these search tools are as reliable as their marketing copy claims. As we've seen throughout this study, many engineering decisions are not made with much thought to the ethical implications of design decisions. And one reason for this is the lack of education in engineering and computer science curricula around ethics. Alex Ahmen, a doctoral student in Computer Science at Northwestern, told Conger and Metz that in her program of study "we're not given an ethics course. We're not given a political education. It's impossible for us to do this [talk about ethics]

60 Lohr, *Data-ism*, 195.

61 O'Neil, *Weapons of Math Destruction*, 208.

62 Kerstin Denecke, "Diversity-Aware Search: New Possibilities and Challenges for Web Search," in *Web Search Engine Research*, ed. Dirk Lewandowski (Emerald Publishing Ltd, 2012), 152.

unless we create the conversations for ourselves."[63] It's no wonder that engineers and designers, who lack this kind of training in their professional programs, fail to integrate these kinds of practices in their daily work once they leave school.

But there is some hope here. Journalist Natasha Singer writes about the current push to create ethics classes in universities, particularly after the effects of technological innovation have become more clear over the past few years. Some schools favor a "medicine-like morality,"[64] but ultimately the idea is to get engineers to start asking questions about what the unintended side effects of their creations might be. She writes that schools increasingly want "the next generation of technologists and policymakers to consider the ramifications of innovations—like autonomous weapons or self-driving cars—before those products go on sale."[65]

This problem is also present in current Library and Information Science programs throughout the world. These programs are behind in teaching librarians the engineering skills they need to create the software that is the backbone of the modern library. A cursory glance at a job board for library software developers will show a desire for candidates who possess education and experience in both libraries and software development. The inference is that the library studies themselves will not be enough to develop someone into a full-fledged software developer. Anecdotally, I know of no library developer who learned their craft in an LIS program. But these LIS programs also fail to teach any of the ethical reasoning skills necessary to carefully think through the implications of our choices to create tools, services, or policies, and how those will affect our patrons and users.

But we also have a responsibility to teach our patrons and users to be skeptical of these search tools, and not just in order to drive traffic from general-purpose search engines like Google to library systems. A healthy skepticism of the objectivity claims made by the companies who make algorithmic systems is necessary for a functioning democracy, as our experience in the United States over the past few years has shown. Director of

---

63   Conger and Metz, "Tech Workers Now Want to Know."

64   Natasha Singer, "Universities Rush to Roll Out Computer Science Ethics Courses," *New York Times,* February 12, 2018, https://www.nytimes.com/2018/02/12/business/computer-science-ethics-courses.html.

65   Singer.

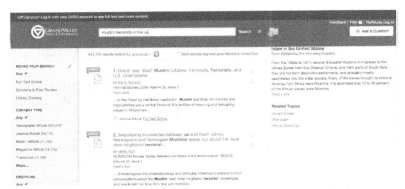

Figure 6.2   Search for muslim terrorist in the united states returns "Islam in the United States"

Teaching and Learning at the University of California, Riverside Library Dani Brecher Cook wrote about the implications of bias in library discovery systems for information literacy education, arguing that "the whole 'Internet=bad, Library=good' dichotomy that is so easy to fall into"[66] is bad for users. Cook pushes us, saying

> If our job is to teach students to be critical consumers and creators of information, I'd say that it's incumbent upon us not to take the easier path, but to surface the way these systems are constructed and the potential for bias and leading that such systems create.[67]

We already teach information literacy skills around evaluation, but its usually in the context of a specific kind of search tool. If you're in Google, we emphasize evaluating the source material. Is this scholarly? What makes you feel you can trust it? In library search tools, on the other hand, we generally breeze past this form of evaluation, arguing that the vendors who compile scholarly sources have done much of this evaluation for us. But as

---

66   Dani Brecher Cook, "Information Literacy Implications of 'Algorithmic Bias in Library Discovery Systems,'" March 14, 2016, https://rulenumberoneblog.com/2016/03/14/information-literacy-implications-of-algorithmic-bias-in-library-discovery-systems/.

67   Cook.

transgender

359,592 results sorted by relevance ▾ 🔊

Add results |

RSS 2.0 feed for current search

1   online

   Transgender
   by Trangadia, M.M. Gupta, B.D.

   Anil Aggrawal's Internet Journal of Forensic Medicine and Toxicology, 01/2013, Volume 14, Issue 1

   Journal Article Full Text Online

   Preview ▾

Figure 6.3 Summon search results for "transgender" search. Screen shot by Regina Gong of Lansing Community College.

we have seen, this is not always true. Oftentimes algorithms amplify social bias, conflating terms in ways that reflect sexist, racist, or other hateful views. The Summon search for "muslim terrorist in the united states," shown in Figure 6.2 and in Chapter 5, returns a Wikipedia article on "Islam in the United States" that implies that *all* muslims in the United States are terrorists. (The autosuggest result for "muslims are" also recommends the search "muslims are terrorists.) In early 2017, a simple keyword query for "transgender" in Summon returned as the first result in many libraries' instances an article from an Internet forensics journal showing crime scene photos of the corpse of a man dressed as a woman (Figure 6.3).[68] A transgender person is not a man wearing women's clothes, so in addition to the graphic nature of these images there was inaccuracy around a socially contentious identity issue. Why was this result the first one Summon showed, when the scholarly import of the publication was not clear, and the accuracy and usefulness of the content were so far off the mark? Ex Libris moved quickly to block the result after it was reported on the Summon Clients' listserv by librarian Sommer Browning of Denver's Auraria Library.[69] But

---

68   Within a week, the Ex Libris team had worked to block this result from its index, although it was not clear if the result was also removed from Gale's Academic OneFile, the subscription database that it was a part of. The result can still be seen at http://anilaggrawal.com/ij/vol_014_no_001/poster/poster007.html, although be warned that the photos are graphic.

69   Sommer Browning, Email to Summon listserv, April 7, 2017, https://exlibrisusers.org/private/summon/2017-April/005379.html.

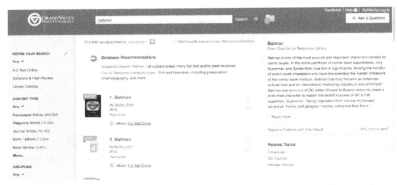

Figure 6.4 Summon Topic Explorer with design changes to give contextual information about the Topic Explorer.

again Ex Libris treated this as an isolated technical issue, rather than a lack of moral imagination on the part of the creators and maintainers of the library discovery system.

One other way to teach users is through changing the design of the system's user interface. After my first round of testing Summon's Topic Explorer, I added a section under each encyclopedia entry to help give users context for why this result appeared on the results page and also a way to report if the result was inaccurate or inappropriate (Figure 6.4). Galvan has criticized this approach, noting that this delegates the burden of quality control for search results from a for-profit company to the library's staff and patrons.[70]

Yet my purpose for designing these features into Summon wasn't just about getting users to report a problem. While there certainly were practical applications for this additional contextual information, the links to report problems and understand why a result might appear also served to intentionally undermine the objectivity and neutrality claims of the discovery system.

---

70   Galvan, "Architecture of Authority."

Conclusion

As we have seen, the claims of objectivity and neutrality in library discovery tools (and algorithmic systems in general) are unwarranted. Even when an algorithm has a high rate of returning successful results, inaccuracies and bias can creep in. When those problematic results are covered over by arguments for the infallibility and objectivity of the algorithm, then deep-seated social prejudices and biases are interpreted as objective truth. These systems have been masked for too long by our trust; it is time we put them in their place.

We must be mindful that these biased and incorrect results from algorithmic systems are not just bugs or glitches in a technological system. Rather, as many of the scholars I have cited throughout this work remind us, algorithms must be understood in their cultural, social, and historical context. Problematic results for searches about marginalized people do not *only* reinforce racist and sexist and homophobic and hateful ideology—they have real affects on marginalized people in the world. These problematic results not only reflect poorly on the objectivity and neutrality claims of libraries, they hurt and hinder our users.

We must call for changes to our algorithmic systems in libraries. We must stop the marketing of our search tools as objective systems, and we must push back against the subtle co-opting of Google's claims for objectivity through mimicking their simplified design patterns. We must not only speak to the shortcomings of algorithmic systems, we must design our systems in such a way that we are not baking assumptions about the infallibility and objectivity of algorithms into the tools. And we must continue to teach librarians, developers, and users to be more critical of algorithmic systems in our lives.

Not all of us are in positions where we can make change in the design and functioning of algorithmic systems. At GVSU, we do not have very robust infrastructure for software development, and we only have two employees (counting me) who write code and design technical systems as part of their regular workload. This is not unusual, and in fact most libraries have even fewer resources than we do. But even when we rely on hosted third-party systems, we can affect change. During the licensing negotiations, push your vendors or your colleagues who negotiate with them to reassess their algorithmic systems in light of the problems I have presented here. Often these systems allow you to make changes to the functioning of one or more algorithms. Here at GVSU, after a period of several years of studying the problems around Summon's Topic Explorer, we decided to turn off the entire Summon sidebar and all of its accessory algorithms like Topic Explorer and recommended topics, librarians, and guides. On March 4th, 2019, I shut off the sidebar for good. We made this choice for our users, so they would be exposed to fewer problematic algorithmic results from the Topic Explorer and other recommendation tools. But we still have the auto-suggest algorithms, and related searches to contend with. The other side of our decision was to send a message to Ex Libris that the way they are treating these problematic algorithms is not acceptable. We will not wait forever to have them take the dissemination of racist, homophobic, transphobic, Islamaphobic, sexist, and otherwise hateful results seriously.

The sidebar has only been off a few days as I write this. I don't know how it will affect our users to be left without contextual information in their searches. I suspect, honestly, that many will not notice. But since the Topic Explorer was launched in 2013, Google's Knowledge Graph and similar contextual algorithms in general-purpose search tools have become the norm. Will the lack of these additional results further distance our users from trusting our library search tools? Will they find them less useful, or find themselves questioning the value of such a basic search engine?

As I ask myself these questions, another question emerges, one that I struggle at times to give voice to. Yet one, in light of the work I have done in this study, that needs to be asked: Would it be so bad if our users questioned the value of our search tools?

Bibliography

"2017 Edelman Trust Barometer—Global Results." Slideshare. Last modified January 15, 2017. https://www.slideshare.net/EdelmanInsights/2017-edelman-trust-barometer-global-results-71035413.

Abrams, Rachel. "Google Thinks I'm Dead. (I Know Otherwise.)." *New York Times,* December 16, 2017. https://www.nytimes.com/2017/12/16/business/google-thinks-im-dead.html.

Albright, Jonathan. "#NotOKGoogle Search Suggestions: 2018 Edition." *Medium* (blog), February 21, 2018. https://medium.com/@d1gi/notokgoogle-search-suggestions-2018-edition-ba09eaf49fc2.

Ananny, Mike. "The Curious Connection Between Apps for Gay Men and Sex Offenders." *The Atlantic,* April 14, 2011. https://www.theatlantic.com/technology/archive/2011/04/the-curious-connection-between-apps-for-gay-men-and-sex-offenders/237340/.

Anderson, Stephen P. "Towards an Ethics of Persuasion." *Ux Mag,* December 13, 2011. http://uxmag.com/articles/towards-an-ethics-of-persuasion.

Angwin, Julia, Jeff Larson, Surya Mattu, and Lauren Kirchner. "Machine Bias: There's Software Used Across the Country to Predict Future Criminals. And it's Biased Against Blacks." *Propublica,* May 23, 2016. https://www.propublica.org/article/machine-bias-risk-assessments-in-criminal-sentencing.

Angwin, Julia, and Surya Mattu. "Amazon Says It Puts Customers First. But its Pricing Algorithm Doesn't." *ProPublica,* September 20, 2016. https://www.propublica.org/article/amazon-says-it-puts-customers-first-but-its-pricing-algorithm-doesnt.

"Article Development." Wikipeda. Last modified March 9, 2018. https://en.wikipedia.org/wiki/Wikipedia:Article_development.

Asher, Andrew, Lynda M. Duke, and Suzanne Wilson. "Paths of Discovery: Comparing the Search Effectiveness of EBSCO Discovery Service, Summon, Google Scholar, and Conventional Library Resources." *College and Research Libraries* 74, no. 5 (2013): 464–83.

Baker, Paul, and Amanda Potts. "'Why Do White People Have Thin Lips?' Google and the Perpetuation of Stereotypes Via Auto-complete Search Forms." *Critical Discourse Studies* 10, no. 2 (2013): 187–204.

Bakshy, Eytan, Itamar Rosenn, Cameron Marlow, and Lada Adamic. "The Role of Social Networks in Information Diffusion." *Proceedings of the 21st International Conference on World Wide Web*. April 2012. https://dl.acm.org/citation.cfm?doid=2187836.2187907.

Barron, Simon, and Andrew Preater. "Critical Systems Librarianship." In *The Politics and the Practice of Critical Librarianship*, edited by Karen P. Nicholson and Maura Seale, 87–113. Sacramento, CA: Library Juice Press, 2018.

Battelle, John. "The Database of Intentions." *John Battelle's Search Blog,* November 13, 2003. https://battellemedia.com/archives/2003/11/the_database_of_intentions.

Beer, David. "The Social Power of Algorithms." *Information, Communication & Society* 20, no. 1 (2017): 1–13.

Beer, Stafford. "What is Cybernetics?," *Kybernetes* 31, no. 2 (2002): 209–19.

Berlatsky, Noah. "Google Search Algorithms are Not Impartial. They Can Be Biased, Just Like Their Designers." *NBC News: Think,* February 21, 2018. https://www.nbcnews.com/think/opinion/google-search-algorithms-are-not-impartial-they-are-biased-just-ncna849886.

Block, Laszlo. "Getting to Work on Diversity at Google." *Google Official Blog,* May 28, 2014. https://googleblog.blogspot.com/2014/05/getting-to-work-on-diversity-at-google.html.

Bogost, Ian. "The Cathedral of Computation." *The Atlantic,* January 15, 2015. https://www.theatlantic.com/technology/archive/2015/01/the-cathedral-of-computation/384300/.

Boguslaw, Robert. "Systems of Power and the Power of Systems." In *Information Technology in a Democracy,* edited by Alan F. Westin, 419–31. Cambridge, MA: Harvard University Press, 1971.

Bolukbasi, Tolga, Kai-Wei Chang, James Zou, Venkatesh Saligrama, and Adam Kalai. "Man is to Computer Programmer as Woman is to Homemaker? Debiased Word Embeddings." (2016). https://arxiv.org/abs/1607.06520.

Bond, Robert M., Christopher J. Fariss, Jason J. Jones, Adam D.I. Kramer, Cameron Marlow, Jaime E. Settle, and James H. Fowler. "A 61-million-person Experiment in Social Influence and Political Mobilization." *Nature* 489, no. 7415 (2012). https://www.ncbi.nlm.nih.gov/pmc/articles/PMC3834737/.

Bourg, Chris. "For the Love of Baby Unicorns." 2018 Code4Lib Conference, February 14, 2018. https://2018.code4lib.org/keynotes/Chris-Bourg.

Bozdag, Engin, and Ibo van de Poel. "Designing for Diversity in Online News Recommenders." *2013 Proceedings of PICMET '13: Technology Management for Emerging Technolgies.* (2013): 1101–1106.

Breeding, Marshall. "Web-Scale Discovery Services: Finding the Right Balance." *American Libraries,* January 14, 2014. https://americanlibrariesmagazine.org/2014/01/14/web-scale-discovery-services/.

Breland, Ali. "White Code, Black Faces." *Logic* 3 (2018): 195–203.

Brin, Sergey, and Larry Page. "The Anatomy of a Large-Scale Hypertextual Web Search Engine." *Computer Networks and ISDN Systems* 30, no. 1 (1998). http://infolab.stanford.edu/~backrub/google.html.

Broussard, Meredith. *Artificial Unintelligence: How Computers Misunderstand the World.* Cambridge, MA: MIT Press, 2018.

Bucher, Tania. "Want to Be on the Top? Algorithmic Power and the Threat of Invisibility on Facebook." *New Media & Society* 14, no. 7 (2012): 1164–1180. https://doi.org/10.1177%2F1461444812440159.

Buolamwini, Joy. "How I'm Fighting Bias in Algorithms." *TED,* November 2016. https://www.ted.com/talks/joy_buolamwini_how_i_m_fighting_bias_in_algorithms.

Burke, Jane. "Discovery Versus Disintermediation: The New Reality Driven by Today's End-User." Paper presented at the VALA Conference, Melbourne, Australia. February, 2010. http://www.vala.org.au/vala2010/papers2010/VALA2010_57_Burke_Final.pdf.

Cadwalladr, Carole. "Google, Democracy and the Truth About Internet Search." *The Guardian,* December 4, 2016. https://www.theguardian.com/technology/2016/dec/04/google-democracy-truth-internet-search-facebook.

————. "How to Bump Holocaust Deniers Off Google's Top Spot? Pay Google." *The Guardian,* December 17, 2016. https://www.theguardian.com/technology/2016/dec/17/holocaust-deniers-google-search-top-spot.

Chen, Sophia. "AI Research Is in Desperate Need of an Ethical Watchdog." *WIRED,* September 18, 2017. https://www.wired.com/story/ai-research-is-in-desperate-need-of-an-ethical-watchdog/.

Christian, Brian, and Tom Griffiths. *Algorithms to Live By: The Computer Science of Human Decisions.* New York: Henry Holt, 2017.

"Christopher Lee: History." Wikipedia. Last modified June 11, 2015. https://en.wikipedia.org/w/index.php?title=Christopher_Lee&oldid=666471973.

Ciccone, Karen, and John Vickery. "Summon, EBSCO Discovery Service, and Google Scholar: A Comparison of Search Performance Using User Queries." *Evidence Based Library and Information Practice* 10, no. 1 (2015): 34–49.

Clancy, Eileen. Twitter Post. March 11, 2018, 5:56pm. https://twitter.com/clancynewyork/status/972999819697455104.

"Code4Lib Community Statement in Support of Chris Bourg." Github: Code4Lib. Accessed February 21, 2019. https://github.com/code4lib/c4l18-keynote-statement.

Conger, Kate, and Cade Metz. "Tech Workers Now Want to Know: What Are We Building This For?" *New York Times,* October 7, 2018. https://www.nytimes.com/2018/10/07/technology/tech-workers-ask-censorship-surveillance.html.

Conger, Kate, and Daisuke Wakabayashi. "Google Overhauls Sexual Misconduct Policy After Employee Walkout." *New York Times,* November 8, 2018. https://www.nytimes.com/2018/11/08/technology/google-arbitration-sexual-harassment.html/.

Cook, Dani Brecher. "Information Literacy Implications of 'Algorithmic Bias in Library Discovery Systems.'" *Rule Number One Blog,* March 14, 2016. https://rulenumberoneblog.com/2016/03/14/information-literacy-implications-of-algorithmic-bias-in-library-discovery-systems/.

Cook, James. "The YouTube Kids App Has Been Suggesting a Load of Conspiracy Videos to Children." *Business Insider,* March 17, 2018. https://www.businessinsider.com/youtube-suggested-conspiracy-videos-to-children-using-its-kids-app-2018-3/?op=1.

Davis, Stephen Paul. "HILCC, a Hierarchical Interface to Library of Congress Classification." *Journal of Internet Cataloging* 5, no. 4 (2002): 19–49.

Denecke, Kerstin. "Diversity-Aware Search: New Possibilities and Challenges for Web Search." In *Web Search Engine Research,* edited by Dirk Lewandowski, 139–62. Emerald Publishing Ltd, 2012.

"Discovery System." Wikipedia. Last Modified September 11, 2017. https://en.wikipedia.org/wiki/Discovery_system.

"Diversity Counts." American Library Association. Last modified 2012. http://www.ala.org/aboutala/offices/diversity/diversitycounts/divcounts.

Dormehl, Luke. *The Formula: How Algorithms Solve All Our Problems—and Create More.* New York: Penguin, 2014.

Dourish, Paul. "Algorithms and Their Others: Algorithmic Culture in Context." *Big Data & Society* 3, no. 2 (2016): 1–11.

Dowd, Maureen. "Soothsayer in the Hills Sees Silicon Valley's Sinister Side." *New York Times,* November 8, 2017. https://www.nytimes.com/2017/11/08/style/jaron-lanier-new-memoir.html.

Dwoskin, Elizabeth. "How Social Bias Creeps Into Web Technology: Software Can Lead to Unintended Errors, Potentially Unfair Outcomes." *Wall Street Journal,* August 21, 2015. https://www.wsj.com/articles/computers-are-showing-their-biases-and-tech-firms-are-concerned-1440102894.

Dwyer, Jim. "A Push to Expose the Computing Process in City Decision-Making." *New York Times,* August 24, 2017. https://www.nytimes.com/2017/08/24/nyregion/showing-the-algorithms-behind-new-york-city-services.html.

"EBSCO Discovery Service (EDS)—Discipline Limited Searching." EBSCO Connect. Last modified October 18, 2018. https://connect.ebsco.com/s/article/EBSCO-Discovery-Service-EDS-Discipline-Limited-Searching?language=en_US.

"EBSCO License Agreement." EBSCO. Accessed February 12, 2019. https://www.ebsco.com/terms-of-use.

"EBSCO Open Collaboration Policy for Technical Interoperability and Bibliographic Record Sharing." EBSCO. Last modified June 2018. https://www.ebsco.com/open-collaboration-policy.

Edelman, Benjamin, and Benjamin Lockwood. "Measuring Bias in "Organic" Web Search." Ben Edelman. January 9, 2011. http://www.benedelman.org/searchbias/.

Editorial Board, The. "A Fight Over 'Aliens'." *New York Times,* June 20, 2016. https://www.nytimes.com/2016/06/20/opinion/a-fight-over-aliens.html.

Ekström, Andreas. "The Moral Bias Behind Your Search Results." *TED,* January 2015. https://www.ted.com/talks/andreas_ekstrom_the_moral_bias_behind_your_ search_results.

"Encyclopædia Britannica: Print Encyclopaedia." Encyclopædia Britannica. Accessed October 13, 2018. https://www.britannica.com/topic/Encyclopaedia-Britannica-print-encyclopaedia.

Epstein, Robert, and Ronald Robertson. "The Search Engine Manipulation Effect (SEME) and Its Possible Impact on the Outcomes of Elections." *Proceedings of the National Academy of Sciences of the United States* 112, no. 33 (2015): E4512-E4521.

Eslami, Motahhare, Aimee Rickman†, Kristen Vaccaro, Amirhossein Aleyasen, Andy Vuong Karrie Karahalios, Kevin Hamilton, and Christian Sandvig. "'I Always Assumed That I Wasn't Really Close to [Her]': Reasoning About Invisible Algorithms in News Feeds." *33rd Annual ACM Conference on Human Factors in Computing Systems.* (2015): 153–62.

Eubanks, Virginia. *Automating Inequality: How High-Tech Tools Profile, Police, and Punish the Poor.* New York: St. Martin's Press, 2017.

Executive Office of the President. *Big Data: Seizing Opportunities, Preserving Values.* May 1, 2014. https://obamawhitehouse.archives.gov/sites/default/files/docs/big_ data_privacy_report_may_1_2014.pdf.

Fallows, Deborah. "Search Engine Users: Internet Searchers Are Confident, Satisfied and Trusting—but They Are Also Unaware and Naïve." *Pew Internet and American Life Project.* January 23, 2005. http://pewinternet.org/Reports/2005/Search-Engine-Users/8-Conclusions/Conclusions.aspx.

Farr, Christina. "Report: Facebook Tested User Loyalty by Sabotaging Its Android App." *Fast Company,* January 4, 2016. https://www.fastcompany.com/3055089/report-facebook-tested-user-loyalty-by-sabotaging-its-android-app.

Feuz, Martin, Matthew Fuller, and Felix Stalder. "Personal Web Searching in the Age of Semantic Capitalism: Diagnosing the Mechanisms of Personalization." *First Monday* 16, no. 2 (2011). http://firstmonday.org/ojs/index.php/fm/article/ view/3344/2766.

Fisher, Ann. "All Sides With Ann Fisher: Tech Tuesday: Cybersecurity at the Olympics, Search Engine Bias." February 13, 2018. http://radio.wosu.org/post/tech-tuesday-cybersecurity-olympics-search-engine-bias#stream/0.

Fister, Barbara. "The Bigot in the Machine." *Inside Higher Ed: Babelfish* (blog), March 17, 2016. https://www.insidehighered.com/blogs/library-babel-fish/bigot-machine.

Foster, Anita K., and Jean B. MacDonald. "A Tale of Two Discoveries: Comparing the Usability of Summon and EBSCO Discovery Service." *Journal of Web Librarianship* 7, no. 1 (2013): 1–19. https://doi.org/10.1080/193222909.2013.757936.

Fry, Hannah. *Hello World: Being Human in the Age of Algorithms.* New York: W.W. Norton, 2018.

Galvan, Angela. "Architecture of Authority." *Angela Fixes Things* (blog), December 5, 2016. https://asgalvan.com/2016/12/05/architecture-of-authority.

Gershgorn, Dave. "Facebook Says It Has a Tool to Detect Bias in Its Artificial Intelligence." *Quartz,* May 3, 2018. https://qz.com/1268520/facebook-says-it-has-a-tool-to-detect-bias-in-its-artificial-intelligence/.

Gillespie, Tarleton. "Can an Algorithm Be Wrong?" *Limn* 1, no. 2 (2012). https://limn.it/can-an-algorithm-be-wrong/.

———. "The Relevance of Algorithms." In *Media Technologies: Essays on communication, materiality, and society,* edited by Tarleton Gillespie, Pablo J. Boczkowski, and Kirsten A. Foot, 167–94. Cambridge, MA: MIT Press, 2014.

———. Twitter Post. March 21, 2018, 6:53am. https://twitter.com/TarletonG/status/976456851025006592.

Goffey, Andrew. "Algorithm." In *Software Studies: A Lexicon,* edited by Matthew Fuller, 15–20. Cambridge, MA: MIT Press, 2008.

"Google Apologises for Photos App's Racist Blunder." *BBC News.* July 1, 2015. https://www.bbc.com/news/technology-33347866.

Graham, David A. "The White-Supremicist Group That Inspired a Racist Manifesto." *The Atlantic,* June 22, 2015. https://www.theatlantic.com/politics/archive/2015/06/council-of-conservative-citizens-dylann-roof/396467/.

Greenfield, Adam. *Radical Technologies: The Design of Everyday Life.* London: Verso, 2017.

Guinee, Kathleen, Maya Eagleton, and Tracy E. Hall. "Adolescents' Internet Search Strategies: Drawing Upon Familiar Cognitive Paradigms When Accessing Electronic Information Sources." *Journal of Educational Computing Research* 29, no. 3 (2003): 363–74.

Halavais, Alex. *Search Engine Society*. Cambridge, UK: Polity, 2009.

Hall, Erica. *Just Enough Research*. New York: A Book Apart, 2013.

Hanson, Cody, Shane Nackerud, and Kristi Jensen. "Affinity Strings: Enterprise Data for Resource Recommendations." *Code4Lib Journal* 5 (December 15, 2008). https://journal.code4lib.org/articles/501.

Hern, Alex. "Flickr Faces Complaints Over 'Offensive' Auto-Tagging for Photos." *The Guardian,* May 20, 2015. https://www.theguardian.com/technology/2015/may/20/flickr-complaints-offensive-auto-tagging-photos.

Hoeppner, Athena. "The Ins and Outs of Evaluating Web-Scale Discovery Services." *Information Today,* April 2012. http://www.infotoday.com/cilmag/apr12/Hoeppner-Web-Scale-Discovery-Services.shtml.

"How Search Algorithms Work." Google Search. Accessed January 4, 2019. https://www.google.com/search/howsearchworks/algorithms/.

"How Search Works." Google Search. Accessed December 11, 2018. https://www.google.com/search/howsearchworks/.

Hutson, Matthew. "Artificial Intelligence Could Identify Gang Crimes—and Ignite an Ethical Firestorm." *Science,* February 28, 2018. https://www.sciencemag.org/news/2018/02/artificial-intelligence-could-identify-gang-crimes-and-ignite-ethical-firestorm.

"Indexing." VuFind. Last modified April 21, 2017. https://vufind.org/wiki/indexing.

"Internet Live Stats." Internet Live Stats. Accessed October 1, 2018. http://www.internetlivestats.com/.

"Introducing the Knowledge Graph: Things, Not Strings." *Google Blog.* May 16, 2012. https://googleblog.blogspot.com/2012/05/introducing-knowledge-graph-things-not.html.

"Introduction to WorldCat Discovery." OCLC. Last modified December 23, 2018. https://help.oclc.org/Discovery_and_Reference/WorldCat_Discovery/Get_started/Introduction_to_WorldCat_Discovery_video.

Isaac, Mike, and Sheera Frenkel. "Facebook Security Breach Exposes Accounts of 50 Million Users." *New York Times,* September 28, 2018. https://www.nytimes.com/2018/09/28/technology/facebook-hack-data-breach.html.

Joachims, Thorsten, Laura Granka, Bing Pan, Helene Hembrooke, Filip Radlinski, and Geri Gay. "Evaluating the Accuracy of Implicit Feedback From Clicks and Query Reformulations in Web Search." *ACM Transactions on Information Systems* 25, no. 2 (2007): 1–27.

Jobin, Anna, and Malte Ziewitz. "Organic Search: How Metaphors Help Cultivate the Web." Alexander Von Humbolt Institut Für Internet und Gesellschaft. March 6, 2018. https://www.hiig.de/en/organic-search-metaphors-help-cultivate-web/.

Kammerer, Yvonne, and Peter Gerjets. "How Search Engine Users Evaulate and Select Web Search Results: The Impact of Seach Engine Interface on Credibility Assessments." In *Web Search Engine Research,* edited by Dirk Lewandowski, 251–79. Emerald Publishing Limited, 2012.

Kantor, Jody. "Working Anything but 9 to 5: Scheduling Technology Leaves Low-Income Parents With Hours of Chaos." *New York Times,* August 13, 2014. https://www.nytimes.com/interactive/2014/08/13/us/starbucks-workers-scheduling-hours.html.

Karahalios, Karrie. "Algorithm Awareness: How the News Feed on Facebook Decides What You Get to See." *MIT Technology Review,* October 21, 2014. https://www.technologyreview.com/s/531676/algorithm-awareness/.

Kasperkevic, Jana. "Google Says Sorry for Racist Auto-Tag in Photo App." *The Guardian,* July 1, 2015. https://www.theguardian.com/technology/2015/jul/01/google-sorry-racist-auto-tag-photo-app.

Kitchin, Rob. "Thinking Critically About and Researching Algorithms." *Information, Communication & Society* 20, no. 1 (2017): 14–29.

Klein, Ezra. "How Technology Is Designed to Bring Out the Worst in Us." *Vox,* February 19, 2018. https://www.vox.com/technology/2018/2/19/17020310/tristan-harris-facebook-twitter-humane-tech-time.

Knight, Will. "How to Fix Silicon Valley's Sexist Algorithms." *MIT Technology Review,* November 23, 2016. https://www.technologyreview.com/s/602950/how-to-fix-silicon-valleys-sexist-algorithms/.

Kovach, Steve. "YouTube and Facebook Promoted a Right-Wing Conspiracy About a Florida Shooting Survivor." *Business Insider,* February 21, 2018. https://www.businessinsider.com/youtube-promotes-conspiracy-theory-video-florida-shooting-survivor-david-hogg-2018-2?r=UK&IR=T.

Kramer, Adam D.I., Jamie E. Guillory, and Jeffrey T. Hancock. "Emotional Contagion Through Social Networks." *Proceedings of the National Academy of Sciences* 111, no.24 (2014): 8788–90.

Lambrecht, Anja, and Catherine E. Tucker. "Algorithmic Bias? An Empirical Study Into Apparent Gender-Based Discrimination in the Display of STEM Career Ads." March 9, 2018. http://dx.doi.org/10.2139/ssrn.2852260.

Lanclos, Donna, and Andrew Asher. "'Ethnographish': The State of the Ethnography in Libraries." *Weave Journal of Library User Experience* 1, no. 5 (October 2016). http://dx.doi.org/10.3998/weave.12535642.0001.503.

Latour, Bruno, and Steve Woolgar. *Laboratory Life: The Construction of Scientific Facts*. Princeton, NJ: Princeton University Press, 1986.

Lepore, Jill. "Baby Doe: A Political History of Tragedy." *The New Yorker,* February 1, 2016. 46–57.

Levin, Sam. "Google Search Results for Abortion Services Promote Anti-Abortion Centers." *The Guardian,* February 13, 2018. https://www.theguardian.com/world/2018/feb/13/abortions-near-me-google-search-results-anti-pro-life-groups-promote.

Lewis, Paul. "'Our Minds Can Be Hijacked': The Tech Insiders Who Fear a Smartphone Dystopia." *The Guardian,* October 6, 2017. https://www.theguardian.com/technology/2017/oct/05/smartphone-addiction-silicon-valley-dystopia.

libraryuopx. "Why the University Library Is Better Than Google for Research!" YouTube Video. 2:11. October 28, 2014. https://www.youtube.com/watch?v=G3yE2E-9zlo.

Lohr, Steve. *Data-Ism: The Revolution Transforming Decision Making, Consumer Behavior, and Almost Everything Else*. New York: Harper Business, 2015.

Lomas, Natasha. "FaceApp Apologizes for Building a Racist AI." *TechCrunch,* April 25, 2017. https://techcrunch.com/2017/04/25/faceapp-apologises-for-building-a-racist-ai/.

Losse, Katherine. *The Boy Kings: A Journey to the Heart of the Social Network*. New York: Free Press, 2014.

Lumb, David. "Read Google's Defensive Response To European Antitrust Charges." *Fast Company,* April 16, 2015. https://www.fastcompany.com/3045132/read-googles-defensive-response-to-european-antitrust-charges.

MacCormick, John. *9 Algorithms That Changed the Future: The Ingenious Ideas That Drive Today's Computers*. Princeton, NJ: Princeton University Press, 2012.

Manjoo, Faheed. "Can Facebook Fix Its Own Worst Bug?" *New York Times,* April 25, 2017. https://www.nytimes.com/2017/04/25/magazine/can-facebook-fix-its-own-worst-bug.html.

Meredith, Sam. "A.I. Can Detect the Sexual Orientation of a Person Based on One Photo, Research Shows." *CNBC,* September 8, 2017. https://www.cnbc.com/2017/09/08/a-i-can-detect-the-sexual-orientation-of-a-person-based-on-one-photo-research-shows.html.

Mann, Merlin. Twitter Post. April 15, 2011, 11:46am. https://twitter.com/hotdogsladies/status/58964552993357825.

Marshall, Joan K. "LC Labeling: An Indictment." In *Revolting Librarians,* edited by Celeste West and Elizabeth Katz, 45–48. San Francisco: Booklegger Press, 1972.

Meyer, Eric, and Sara Wachter-Boettcher. *Design for Real Life.* New York: A Book Apart, 2016.

Mitra, Ambarish. "We Can Train AI to Identify Good and Evil, and Then Use It to Teach Us Morality." *Quartz,* April 5, 2018. https://qz.com/1244055/we-can-train-ai-to-identify-good-and-evil-and-then-use-it-to-teach-us-morality/.

Mittelstadt, Brent Daniel, Patrick Allo, Mariarosaria Taddeo, Sandra Wachter, and Luciano Floridi. "The Ethics of Algorithms: Mapping the Debate." *Big Data & Society* 3, no. 2 (2016): 1–21. https://doi.org/10.1177/2053951716679679.

Mowshowitz, Abbe, and Akira Kawaguchi. "Assessing Bias in Search Engines." *Information Processing and Management* 38, no. 1 (2013): 141–56.

Murdoch, Iris. *Existentialists and Mystics: Writings on Philosophy and Literature.* New York: Allen Lane/Penguin Press, 1997.

Nafus, Dawn, Bernhard Kreiger, and James Leach. "Gender: Integrated Report of Findings." *Free/Libre and Open Source Software: Policy Support.* March 1, 2006. http://flosspols.merit.unu.edu/deliverables/FLOSSPOLS-D16-Gender_Integrated_Report_of_Findings.pdf.

Narayanan, Arvind. Twitter Post. August 27, 2017, 9:57am. https://twitter.com/random_walker/status/901851127624458240.

———. Twitter Post. March 20, 2018, 8:25am. https://twitter.com/random_walker/status/976117562500055040.

Nardi, Bonnie A., and Vicki L. O'Day. *Information Ecologies: Using Technology With Heart.* Cambridge, MA: MIT Press, 1999.

Newitz, Annalee. "Princeton Researchers Discover Why AI Become Racist and Sexist." *Ars Technica,* April 18, 2017. https://arstechnica.com/science/2017/04/princeton-scholars-figure-out-why-your-ai-is-racist/.

Nicas, Jack. "Apple's Radical Approach to News: Humans Over Machines." *New York Times,* October 25, 2018. https://www.nytimes.com/2018/10/25/technology/apple-news-humans-algorithms.html.

————. "The Week in Tech: Apple Goes on the Attack." *New York Times,* October 26, 2018. https://www.nytimes.com/2018/10/26/technology/apple-time-cook-europe.html.

Noble, Safiya Umoja. "Missed Connections: What Search Engines Say About Women." *Bitch* 1, no. 54 (2012): 36–41.

————. "Google Search: Hyper-Visibility as a Means of Rendering Black Women and Girls Invisible." *InVisible Culture: An Electronic Journal for Visual Culture* 19 (October 29, 2013). https://ivc.lib.rochester.edu/google-search-hyper-visibility-as-a-means-of-rendering-black-women-and-girls-invisible/.

————. *Algorithms of Oppression: How Search Engines Reinforce Racism.* New York: New York University Press, 2018.

Noble, Safiya Umoja, and Sarah T. Roberts. "Engine Failure: Safiya Umoja Noble and Sarah T. Roberts on the Problems of Platform Capitalism." *Logic* 3 (2017): 89–99.

"OCLC WorldCat.org Services Terms and Conditions." OCLC WorldCat. Last modified September 24, 2009. https://www.oclc.org/content/dam/ext-ref/worldcat-org/terms.html.

"Oh, Go to Hell." *Damn You, Autosuggest: Or Primo Knows Best. Auto-Suggest Failures From Library Catalogs and Databases* (blog). March 26, 2015. http://damnyouautosuggest.tumblr.com/post/114699603389/oh-go-to-hell.

Olson, Hope A. *The Power to Name: Locating the Limits of Subject Representation in Libraries.* Dordrecht, Netherlands: Kluwer Academic Publishers, 2002.

O'Neil, Cathy. *Weapons of Math Destruction: How Big Data Increases Inequality and Threatens Democracy.* New York: Crown, 2016.

————. "United Airlines Exposes Our Twisted Idea of Dignity." *Bloomberg*, April 18, 2017. https://www.bloomberg.com/opinion/articles/2017-04-18/united-airlines-exposes-our-twisted-idea-of-dignity.

"Online Databases." East Brunswick Public Library. Accessed October 14, 2018. https://www.ebpl.org/main/online_databases_info.cfm.

"Our Mission." Google Search. Accessed November 10, 2018. https://www.google.com/search/howsearchworks/mission/.

Pande, Vijay. "Artificial Intelligence's 'Black Box' Is Nothing to Fear." *New York Times,* January 25, 2018. https://www.nytimes.com/2018/01/25/opinion/artificial-intelligence-black-box.html.

Pang, Alex Soojung-Kim. *The Distraction Addiction.* New York: Little Brown, 2013.

Pariser, Eli. *The Filter Bubble: How the New Personalized Web Is Changing What We Read and How We Think.* New York: Penguin Books, 2012.

Pasquale, Frank. *The Black Box Society: The Secret Algorithms That Control Money and Information.* Cambridge, MA: Harvard University Press, 2015.

Pattern, Dave. "Relevance Rules." *Self Plagiarism Is Style* (blog), May 6, 2012. https://www.daveyp.com/2012/05/06/relevancy-rules/.

———. "Dumping the OPAC #2—usage Data." *Self Plagiarism Is Style* (blog), May 25, 2013. https://www.daveyp.com/2013/05/25/dumping-the-opac-2-usage-data.

"Personalizing Search Results in Primo VE." Ex Libris Knowledge Center. Accessed February 12, 2019. https://knowledge.exlibrisgroup.com/Primo/Product_Documentation/020Primo_VE/100End_User_Help/015Personalizing_Search_Results_in_Primo_VE.

Powers, William. *Twelve by Twelve: A One-Room Cabin Off the Grid and Beyond the American Dream.* New York: New World Library, 2010.

Powles, Julia. "New York City's Bold, Flawed Attempt to Make Algorithms Accountable." *The New Yorker,* December 20, 2017. https://www.newyorker.com/tech/annals-of-technology/new-york-citys-bold-flawed-attempt-to-make-algorithms-accountable.

"Primo Central Terms of Service." Ex Libris Knowledge Center. Accessed February 12, 2019. https://knowledge.exlibrisgroup.com/Primo/Content_Corner/Product_Documentation/Primo_Central_Terms_of_Service.

"Professional Codes of Ethics for Librarians." IFLA. Last modified June 15, 2017. https://www.ifla.org/faife/professional-codes-of-ethics-for-librarians.

"Professional Ethics." American Library Association. Last modified January 22, 2008. http://www.ala.org/tools/ethics.

Purcell, Kristen, Joanna Brenner, and Lee Rainie. "Search Engine Use 2012." *Pew Internet and American Life Project.* March 9, 2012. Retrieved from http://www.pewinternet.org/2012/03/09/search-engine-use-2012/.

Rabey, Lisa. Twitter Post. March 11, 2018, 5:00pm. https://twitter.com/heroineinabook/status/972985545314971648.

Raicu, Irina. "Autocompleted." *Markkula Center for Applied Ethics,* May 9, 2017. https://www.scu.edu/ethics/internet-ethics-blog/autocompleted/.

Rieh, Soo Young, and Brian Hilligoss. "College Students Credibility Judgments in the Information-Seeking Process." In *Digital Media, Youth, and Credibility,* edited by Miriam J. Metzger and Andrew J. Flanagin, 49–71. Cambridge, MA: MIT Press, 2008.

Robertson, Campbell, Christopher Mele, and Sabrina Taverinse. "11 Killed in Synagogue Massacre; Suspect Charged With 29 Counts." *New York Times,* October 27, 2018. https://www.nytimes.com/2018/10/27/us/active-shooter-pittsburgh-synagogue-shooting.html.

Rucker, Philip. "Amid Incendiary Rhetoric, Targets of Trump's Words Become Targets of Bombs." *Washington Post,* October 24, 2018. https://www.washingtonpost.com/politics/amid-incendiary-rhetoric-targets-of-trumps-words-become-targets-of-bombs/2018/10/24/9dddc97c-d7c7-11e8-83a2-d1c3da28d6b6_story.html.

Sadler, Bess, and Chris Bourg. "Feminism and the Future of Library Discovery." *Code4ib Journal* 28 (2015). https://journal.code4lib.org/articles/10425.

Sacasas, Michael. "The Ethics of Technological Mediation." *The Frailest Thing* (blog), November 18, 2017. https://thefrailestthing.com/2017/11/18/the-ethics-of-technological-mediation/.

Scott, Allison, Freada Kapor Klein, and Uriridiakoghene Onovakpuri. "Tech Leavers Study: A First-Of-Its-Kind Analysis of Why People Voluntarily Left Jobs in Tech." *The Kapor Center for Social Impact,* April 27, 2017. https://www.kaporcenter.org/wp-content/uploads/2017/08/TechLeavers2017.pdf.

"Search Engine Market Share." Net Market Share. Accessed October 1, 2018. https://www.netmarketshare.com/search-engine-market-share.aspx.

Seaver, Nick. "Knowing Algorithms." *Media in Transition* 8 (2013). http://niceseaver.net/papers/seaverMiT8.pdf.

———. "Algorithms as Culture: Some Tactics for the Ethnography of Algorithmic Systems." *Big Data & Society* 4, no. 2 (2017): 1–12.

Siegler, M. G. "Marissa Mayer's Next Big Thing: 'Contextual Discovery'—Google Results Without Search." *TechCrunch,* December 8, 2010. http://techcrunch.com/2010/12/08/googles-next-big-thing.

Simon, Herbert A. "Rational Choice and the Structure of the Environment." *Psychological Review* 63, no. 2 (1956): 129–38.

Simonite, Tom. "Machines Taught by Photos Learn a Sexist View of Women." *WIRED*, August 21, 2017. https://www.wired.com/story/machines-taught-by-photos-learn-a-sexist-view-of-women/.

Singer, Natasha. "Your Online Attention, Bought in an Instant." *New York Times*, November 17, 2012. https://www.nytimes.com/2012/11/18/technology/your-online-attention-bought-in-an-instant-by-advertisers.html.

———. "Universities Rush to Roll Out Computer Science Ethics Courses." *New York Times*, February 12, 2018. https://www.nytimes.com/2018/02/12/business/computer-science-ethics-courses.html.

Solon, Olivia, and Sam Levin. "How Google's Search Algorithm Spreads False Information With a Rightwing Bias." *The Guardian*, December 16, 2016. https://www.theguardian.com/technology/2016/dec/16/google-autocomplete-rightwing-bias-algorithm-political-propaganda.

Sorrel, Charlie. "Self-Driving Mercedes Will Be Programmed to Sacrifice Pedestrians to Save the Driver." *Fast Company*, October 13, 2016. https://www.fastcompany.com/3064539/self-driving-mercedes-will-be-programmed-to-sacrifice-pedestrians-to-save-the-driver.

"Sort by Popularity, Price, or Condition." Amazon Web Services. Accessed October 10, 2018. https://docs.aws.amazon.com/AWSECommerceService/latest/DG/SortingbyPopularityPriceorCondition.html.

"Summon: Add Results Beyond Your Library's Collection." Ex Libris Knowledge Center. Last modified February 21, 2014. https://knowledge.exlibrisgroup.com/Summon/Product_Documentation/Searching_in_The_Summon_Service/Search_Features/Summon%3A_Add_Results_Beyond_Your_Library's_Collection.

"Summon: Disciplines in the Summon Index." Ex Libris Knowledge Center. Last modified February 20, 2014. https://knowledge.exlibrisgroup.com/Summon/Product_Documentation/Searching_in_The_Summon_Service/Search_Results/Summon%3A_Disciplines_in_the_Summon_Index.

"Summon: Index-Enhanced Direct Linking to Provider Content." Ex Libris Knowledge Center. Last modified February 21, 2014. https://knowledge.exlibrisgroup.com/Summon/Product_Documentation/Configuring_The_Summon_Service/Direct_Linking_in_the_Summon_Service/Summon%3A_Index-Enhanced_Direct_Linking_to_Provider_Content.

"Summon: Phrase, Field, Boolean, Wildcard and Proximity Searching." Ex Libris Knowledge Center. Last modified March 24, 2014. https://knowledge.exlibrisgroup. com/Summon/Product_Documentation/Searching_in_The_Summon_Service/ Search_Features/Summon%3A_Boolean%2C_Phrase%2C_Wildcard_and_ Proximity_Searching.

"Summon: Record Contents and Display." Ex Libris Knowledge Center. Last modified August 15, 2016. https://knowledge.exlibrisgroup.com/Summon/Product_ Documentation/Searching_in_The_Summon_Service/Search_Results/ Summon%3A_Record_Contents_and_Display.

"Summon: Topic Explorer" Summon: Product Documentation. Last modified August 25, 2016. https://knowledge.exlibrisgroup.com/Summon/Product_Documentation/ Searching_in_The_Summon_Service/Search_Results/Summon%3A_ Topic_Explorer.

"Summon Topics." Ex Libris Knowledge Center. Accessed February 12, 2019. https:// knowledge.exlibrisgroup.com/Summon/Product_Documentation/Searching_in_ The_Summon_Service/Search_Results/Summon%3A_Summon_Topics.

Sundar, S. Shyam. "The MAIN Model: A Heuristic Approach to Understanding Technology Effects on Credibility." In *Digital Media, Youth, and Credibility*, edited by Miriam J. Metzger and Andrew J. Flanagin, 73–100. Cambridge, MA: MIT Press, 2008.

Sweeney, Latanya. "Discrimination in Online Ad Delivery." *Communications of the ACM* 56, no. 5 (2013): 44–54.

Sweeney, Miriam. "Not Just a Pretty (Inter)face: A Critical Analysis of Microsoft's 'Ms. Dewey'." PhD diss., University of Illinois at Urbana-Champaign, 2013.

Swisher, Kara. "Who Will Teach Silicon Valley to Be Ethical?" *New York Times,* October 21, 2018. https://www.nytimes.com/2018/10/21/opinion/who-will-teach-silicon-valley-to-be-ethical.html.

Tay, Aaron. "How Is Google Different From Traditional Library OPACs & Databases?" *Musings About Librarianship* (blog), May 8, 2012. http://musingsaboutlibrarianship. blogspot.com/2012/05/how-is-google-different-from.html.

———. "Primo and Summon—Same but Different?" *Musings About Librarianship* (blog), February 29, 2016. http://musingsaboutlibrarianship.blogspot.com/2016/02/primo-and-summon-same-but-different-i.html.

Tempelman-Kluit, Nadaleen. Twitter Post. May 10, 2016, 12:25pm. https://twitter.com/ Nadaleen/status/730116596728012800/photo/1.

"Terms of Service." Google. Last modified April 16, 2007. https://tools.google.com/dlpage/ res/webmmf/en/eula.html.

Todd, Michael. "Nick Seaver on Dissecting the Algorithmic Organism." *Method Space,* February 15, 2018. https://www.methodspace.com/nick-seaver-dissecting-algorithmic-organism/.

Torres, Monica. "New App Scans Your Face and Tells Companies Whether You're Worth Hiring." *Ladders,* August 25, 2017. https://www.theladders.com/career-advice/ai-screen-candidates-hirevue.

Tschantz, Michael Carl, Serge Egelman, Jaeyoung Choi, Nicholas Weaver, and Gerald Friedland. "The Accuracy of the Demographic Inferences Shown on Google's Ad Settings." *Tech. Report TR-16-003, International Computer Science Institute, 2016,* October, 2016. https://www1.icsi.berkeley.edu/~mct/pubs/wpes18/.

Tufekci, Zeynep. "The Real Bias Built in at Facebook." *New York Times,* May 19, 2016. https://www.nytimes.com/2016/05/19/opinion/the-real-bias-built-in-at-facebook.html.

————. "YouTube, the Great Radicalizer." *New York Times,* March 10, 2018. https://www.nytimes.com/2018/03/10/opinion/sunday/youtube-politics-radical.html.

————. Twitter Post. March 12, 2018, 9:52am. https://twitter.com/zeynep/status/973240286120878085.

Turkle, Sherry. *Life on the Screen: Identity in the Age of the Internet.* New York: Simon and Schuster, 1997.

"Useful Responses Take Many Forms." Google Search. Accessed January 31, 2019. https://www.google.com/search/howsearchworks/responses/#?modal_active=none.

Vaidhyanathan, Siva. *The Googlization of Everything (And Why We Should Worry).* Berkely: University of California Press, 2011.

Van Halsema, Liz. "Google vs. Library Databases: Which is Better for Research?" SirsiDynix, September 29, 2014. http://www.sirsidynix.com/blog/2014/09/29/google-vs-library-databases-which-is-better-for-research.

Verbeek, Peter-Paul. *Moralizing Technology: Understanding and Designing the Morality of Things.* Chicago: University of Chicago Press, 2011.

Vicens, A.J. "Top Facebook Exec Sheryl Sandberg Just Apologized for Racist Ad Targeting." *Mother Jones,* September 20, 2017. https://www.motherjones.com/politics/2017/09/top-facebook-exec-sheryl-sandberg-just-apologized-for-racist-ad-targeting/.

Wachter-Boettcher, Sara. *Technically Wrong: Sexist Apps, Biased Algorithms, and Other Threats of Toxic Tech.* New York: W.W. Norton, 2017.

————. "Facebook Treats Its Ethical Failures Like Software Bugs, and That's Why They Keep Happening." *Quartz,* October 20, 2017. https://qz.com/1107036/facebook-treats-its-ethical-failures-like-software-bugs-and-thats-why-they-keep-happening/.

Wakabayashi, Daisuke. "Trump Says Google Is Rigged, Despite Its Denials. What Do We Know About How It Works?" *New York Times,* September 5, 2018. https://www. nytimes.com/2018/09/05/technology/google-trump-bias.html.

Wakabayashi, Daisuke, and Cecilia Kang. "It's Google's Turn in Washington's Glare." *New York Times,* September 26, 2018. https://www.nytimes.com/2018/09/26/ technology/google-conservatives-washington.html.

"What is Available in Library Collection Limiter in EBSCO Discovery Service?" EBSCO. Accessed January 17, 2019. https://help.ebsco.com/interfaces/EBSCO_Discovery_ Service/EDS_FAQs/Available_in_Library_Collection_limiter_EDS.

"What is the Difference Between Subject Facets and Subject: Thesaurus Terms Facets?" EBSCO. Accessed October 11, 2018. https://help.ebsco.com/interfaces/ EBSCOhost/EBSCOhost_FAQs/difference_between_Subject_facets_and_ Subject_Thesaurus_Terms_facets.

White, Erin. "Data-Driven Design Decisions for Discovery Interfaces." Presentation at LITA Forum 2012, Columbus, OH. October 6, 2012. https://scholarscompass.vcu. edu/cgi/viewcontent.cgi?article=1006&context=libraries_present.

Whitman, Walt. "Leaves of Grass." *Bartleby.com.* Accessed February 21, 2019. https://www.bartleby.com/142/14.html.

"Why Do I Get an Error Page When Linking Out to EBSCOhost Databases?" Ex Libris Knowledge Center. Last modified May 18, 2017. https://knowledge.exlibrisgroup. com/Summon/Knowledge_Articles/Why_do_I_get_an_error_page_when_ linking_out_to_EBSCOhost_databases.

Wiggers, Kyle. "Microsoft Is Developing a Tool to Help Engineers Catch Bias in Algorithms." *VentureBeat,* May 25, 2018. https://venturebeat.com/2018/05/25/ microsoft-is-developing-a-tool-to-help-engineers-catch-bias-in-algorithms/.

Willson, Michele. "Algorithms (And The) Everyday." *Information, Communication & Society* 20, no. 1 (2017): 137–50.

Winner, Langdon. "Do Artifacts Have Politics?" *Daedalus* 109, no. 1 (1980): 121–36.

Ziewitz, Malte. "Governing Algorithms: Myth, Mess, and Methods." *Science, Technology, & Human Values* 41, no. 1 (2016): 3–16.

Zinoman, Jason. "The Netflix Executives Who Bent Comedy to Their Will." *New York Times,* September 10, 2018. https://www.nytimes.com/2018/09/09/arts/television/ netflix-comedy-strategy-exclusive.html.

Zunger, Yonatan. Twitter Post. June 29, 2015, 11:21am. https://twitter.com/yonatanzunger/ status/615585776110170112.

Index